The Christian Understanding
of Human Nature

THE CHRISTIAN
UNDERSTANDING
OF HUMAN NATURE

by W. Norman Pittenger

THE WESTMINSTER PRESS
Philadelphia

PUBLISHED BY THE WESTMINSTER PRESS ®

PHILADELPHIA 7, PENNSYLVANIA

PRINTED IN THE UNITED STATES OF AMERICA

Dedicated
to
John Knox and Daniel Day Williams
For Many Years
Beloved Friends

Contents

Preface

The chapters in this book are an expansion of lectures delivered in January, 1963, at the Episcopal Seminary of the Caribbean, near San Juan, Puerto Rico, and were also given in their present form as lectures at Ripon Hall, Oxford, England, in September, 1963. I am very grateful to the faculty of the Caribbean seminary for inviting me to inaugurate its visiting lectureship, and to the Reverend W. G. Fallows, Principal of Ripon Hall, for the invitation to give the visiting lectures at that college. I am also grateful to both institutions for their gracious hospitality while the lectures were being delivered.

Much of the material found in this book has been used in other lectures during the years in which it was being prepared. In an earlier form, some of the chapters were lectures at Vassar College, Poughkeepsie, New York, under the auspices of the Department of Religion. The ninth chapter was originally a lecture given at Sarah Lawrence College, Bronxville, New York, in a symposium on " Human Freedom." Other chapters have been used at university conferences in Australia, during my visit there in 1959; at a faculty conference at Amherst College, Massachusetts; and at clergy conferences in Aberystwyth, Wales (for the clergy of the diocese of St. David's), at the College of

Preachers in Washington, D.C., and in the Episcopal dioceses of Chicago and San Joaquin in the United States. Parts of the first chapters in the book were also given as the opening address at the annual conference of Modern Churchmen, held at St. Hilda's College in Oxford in 1961.

My purpose in this book is not to present a complete and systematic doctrine of man. Rather, it is to state and develop certain emphases in the Christian understanding of human nature that are particularly relevant in the contemporary world, with the intention of showing that these emphases are related to, and necessarily imply, the specifically Christian view of God, the world, and the human situation. Over the years I have become more than ever convinced of the validity of the remark by Dr. Georges Florowsky which I quote in the first chapter. An understanding of what man is provides, as he said and as I believe, one of the best approaches to a grasp of the Christian faith in its widest sense; although, as I have argued in the text, the converse is also true — for it is through the insight provided by Christian faith that the most penetrating insight into the meaning of our manhood is made possible.

I have ventured to add a brief appended note on the meaning of words used in Christian worship. My reason is that the question of language is much to the fore in our time, and my continued insistence in the body of the book on the place and value of worship may raise some questions concerning the significance and use of liturgical language. Worship is at the heart of the Christian life and is the enactment of the Christian faith; if worship is, as I have argued, essential to the true well-being of man, it seems proper to give some attention to the way in which words are used, and the meaning which is found in such words, in this central part of the Christian tradition.

It remains to thank the editors of various periodicals in which parts of this book have appeared in the form of essays: *Theology, The Christian Century* (" In Defense of Universal Salvation," June 7, 1961) , *motive* (" The Meaning of Words In Worship," January, 1957) , and *The Living Church*. I also thank Mrs. Mary Miller, who patiently deciphered the nearly illegible first text and typed the fair copy speedily and accurately.

W. N. P.

1

Introduction: *What Is Man?*

Man has always been a problem to himself. Who is he? What is he *for?* What can he make of himself? Does he count for anything in the scheme of things? Is his significance limited to what can be contained in the conventional threescore and ten years of his life in this world?

The psalmist asks, " What is man? " in the context of a theistic world view, for he goes on to say, " that *thou* art mindful of him? " Many today ask this same question in the context of a nontheistic world view or one that is at best doubtfully theistic. But whatever the context, the problem of man is perennial to himself. And it may be, indeed it is the contention of this book that it is, the fact that the only understanding of human nature adequate to what we know about ourselves implies not merely a theistic context but much more radically a Christian context.

Nearly thirty years ago, I attended a conference of the Student Christian Movement at Swanick in England. One of the speakers was Dr. Georges Florowsky, then a young teacher at the Russian Seminary in Paris. I have never forgotten a sentence that occurred in one of his lectures: " You can best understand what is true about God and about everything else, if you first discover what is true about man." This seems to me a very penetrating statement. It is even more true about any religious faith: if you want to know what a given religion, a given faith, believes about God, nature, history, you should first see what it believes about human nature. Nor does this necessarily imply an anthropocentric position that seeks to make man " the measure of all things." It means simply that the way in which man is understood, and his significance determined, will give us as nothing else can do an insight into the setting, historic and cosmic, in which man makes his appearance.

It is for this reason that I believe a discussion of the meaning of man as he is, when seen in the light of Christian thought, will open up to us and involve for us the whole range of Christian faith. When we come to see what human nature is like, in its present condition, its possibilities, its defeats and its triumphs, its faults and its virtues, we shall be better able to grasp what Christian faith has to say about God who is the determiner of man's destiny, about the world in which human existence is set, and about the history of which that existence is part and parcel.

In the contemporary world there are a great many definitions of man, most of them implicit rather than explicit. We hear that man is an economic counter, for instance. He is both agent and victim of the supply-and-demand chain; he is the consumer, whose wants are to be satisfied — and not only satisfied but stimulated by techniques of open advertising and " hidden " persuasion so that production can be maintained and increased. And that is true. But surely man is much more than that; he is not simply an economic counter. Again, we are told that man is a political animal — or better, perhaps, a social animal, which is what Aristotle meant when he began the *Politics* with the description of man as *zōon politikon*. And there can be no question that man is a social animal. He finds himself a member of a social group to which he belongs simply by the fact of his having been born; without such social belonging he would be less than human, more like the " wolf children " in India of whom we heard some years ago. Nor can there be any doubt that man does express himself in political ways, through the established agencies of tribe or city or state. But again these facts hardly exhaust the full meaning of human nature. If they did, men would be more like ants in an anthill than beings possessed of genuine personal identity; they would be, what William Whyte, Jr., fears they are on the way to becoming through the enormous mass pressures of modern life, nothing more than " organization men," pale reflections of the group and its mores. Yet the very protest that this author, and many others, both record and offer indicates that there is something more to man than just that.

Again, we hear much about man as a sexual being, or as a complex psychological being, or even as nothing more than a rather complicated animal whose responses can be manipulated by the employment of discoverable techniques. We are told, too, that he is to be understood simply in terms of the national group to which he belongs: he is an American man, for example, whose entire existence consists in his being a citizen of that given nation or culture, participating in its affairs, loyal to its ideals, entirely submitted to its way of life. Even more terribly, the recent Fascist and Nazi interpretation of human nature, which is not without parallels in contemporary " segregationist " circles, was wholly in terms of what was called " race ": there was Aryan man, for instance, and now in some parts of the world there is " the white man " — and to say this was or is to say the most important, if not the only, thing that could be said about him. None of these descriptions, however, is really adequate. Man is more than a sexual being, he is more than a complex psychological creature, he is more than a complicated beast, and certainly he is more than a specimen of a national culture or an instance of some given race.

We must not overlook an equally partial definition, given often by those who would defend what they conceive to be the religious point of view. For such persons, man is thought to be properly described as a " spiritual being." This definition, which like the rest is partially true and within a wider context has great importance, is perhaps one of the most viciously inadequate of them all when taken in isolation, for it forgets that in our human experience there is no such thing as the *wholly* spiritual. The only human nature we know is an embodied humanity. Man in his own experience is neither an animal nor an angel; he is no more " spiritual man " exclusively than he is " materialistic man " exclusively. In fact he is just *man*.

It is important to notice that all these definitions of man, and many more that resemble them, are inadequate not only because they fail to take into account so much that we see and experience of humanity in the here and now of our present life. They are also inadequate because for the most part they are so completely *contemporary*. They fail to take account of what we might call the " historicity " of man, his rootedness in the past, his sharing in the ongoing life of the race to which he belongs, his projection of himself into the future with all its possibilities and its hopes. Many today seem to have succeeded, in their thinking about themselves and their fellows, in dehistoricizing human nature, deracinating it, uprooting it. Indeed, for them

man is (in the title of Simone Weil's remarkable book)
" without roots." He is for them so much a contemporary
that he seems to be one who wanders about on the earth
but who *belongs* nowhere.

Now it is my contention that the Christian understanding of human nature is drawn from an honest reckoning
with facts that are patent to all of us, once we have gone
deep into our own existence. Such a Christian understanding does not contradict any of the truths that are being
asserted in the other definitions. It only insists that these
definitions are partial, limited, and nothing like adequate
to the rich reality of the being whom they seek to describe.
The Christian would say that these definitions lack " the
dimension of depth," as Berdyaev once put it; they are
surface definitions that do not penetrate sufficiently into
human existence as we know it when we look carefully, un-
flinchingly, and honestly into ourselves. Our greatest danger, these days, is that we may live, and often do live, as if
one or other of these definitions were the whole truth; and
that we come to treat our fellows as if this were all that
could be said about them. Hence we come close to the dehu-
manizing of ourselves and others.

I have said that " we come close " to doing this, for I
gravely doubt whether in actual fact we can accomplish
this ghastly deed. What seems to happen is that when we
treat men as less than men, a protest begins to boil up in
the depths of human existence, sometimes with devastating
consequences once it emerges on the surface. When we take
a sufficiently comprehensive survey of human history, we
observe that men refuse to let themselves be treated in this
way for too long a time. Their human nature reasserts itself, either by patient and continued protest or by some violent and catastrophic irruption. Man is man, not simply

economic counter, nor social animal, nor sexuality incarnate, nor fallen angel, not simply American nor Russian nor German nor Aryan nor white nor black. Man is man; and sooner or later he declares himself as man — and then woe to those who have treated him or who would treat him as less or other than that.

So much for introduction.

But what, then, *is* man? I believe that the Christian view of man is also and at the same time the genuinely humanistic view of man. It is a full and rounded view, taking account of the truths in the several other definitions but also taking account of facts that these other definitions fail to see. The Christian view is humanistic, but it is not to be confused with that facile and popular humanism which disregards both the depths of man's cosmic belonging and the heights of his divine aspiration. In Jacques Maritain's phrases, it is " a true humanism " or " an integral humanism." It is a portrayal of man seen as he really is in the profoundest ranges of his existence, and seen also in the natural, historical, and divine setting in which he does in fact have that existence.

I shall set down here a series of statements that will give us a structure, or schema, for the development, in succeeding chapters, of the view of human nature and its meaning which I believe to be adequate to the facts and which also happens — and I contend that this is in no sense accidental — to reflect the basic affirmations of Christian faith.

1. Man is a creaturely, dependent being; in Christian language, he is made by God. (Chapter 2.)

2. Man is a creature with a purpose that is to be fulfilled; in Christian language, he is made for fellowship with God. (Chapter 2.)

3. Man is created for community with others; in Chris-

tian language, he shares life as a member of the human race who are all of them the children of God. (Chapter 3.)

4. Man is neither soul alone, nor body alone, but body-soul unity; in Christian language, he is made of the dust of the earth, yet has been " breathed " into life by the Spirit of God. (Chapter 3.)

5. Man's nature as " embodied " and man's social " belonging " make it natural that his relationship with God shall be sustained by " sacramental " means; in Christian language, he is to be baptized by " water and the Spirit " and strengthened and nourished by " the spiritual food of Christ's body and blood." (Chapter 4.)

6. Man is a sexual being, whose sexual drives with their expression in sexual relations are integral to his true nature; in Christian language, he is made to love his fellowmen in God and as a sacrament of his relationship with God. (Chapter 5.)

7. Man is in defection from the purpose for which he was created; in Christian language, he is a sinner, estranged from the God for communion with whom he is made. (Chapter 6.)

8. Man has the potentiality of restoration to health or wholeness; in Christian language, he has been " saved " by being established in a right relationship with his Creator and hence into a right relationship with himself and with others, and he can be brought to accept this fact. (Chapter 7.)

9. Man is mortal, but at the same time is not totally fulfilled nor completely explained in terms of this present world; in Christian language, he dies as do all creatures, yet both now in this present life and also after this life he may have the fruition of his God-given potentialities through abiding fellowship with his Maker. (Chapter 8.)

10. In consequence of these facts, man is a moral being and this means that he is also in some profound sense a " free " being with responsibility for his choices. (Chapters 9 and 10.) This corollary of the above nine points is indeed another way of defining man; in Christian language, one might say that he is created with some genuine freedom of choice or (as I think Berdyaev somewhere phrases it) he is to be defined as having " creaturely freedom." Without that or apart from that, nothing of importance can be said about human nature, by the Christian or by anybody else; and it is the merit of the existentialists of our own day, like Heidegger and even Sartre, that they understand and insist on this essential truth about man.

In the chapters that follow, we shall consider these several assertions, in the confidence that they will give us insight not only into the meaning of our own human lives but also into the true significance of some of the central affirmations of Christian faith.

2

Man as Dependent and Unfulfilled

We have said that man is a created being; in the classical theological phrase, he is " a creature." But perhaps it might be better to put this basic fact in yet another way: *Man is a dependent being.* He does not explain himself; he did not bring himself into existence; if he has any significance at all, it is a significance that must be found in his relationship as a being dependent on that which is not man. It is unfortunate that a quite considerable number of our contemporaries in the Western world seem to think that to speak in such a way about man necessarily must imply that one accepts literally and exactly the story of man's creation as it is told in the book of Genesis in the Old Testament. Doubtless this is due to thoroughly bad religious teaching. But of course it is not the case that recognition of man's creaturely dependent status is inseparably linked with Biblical fundamentalism. No intelligent person, no soundly instructed Christian either, is likely to believe these days that the stories in Genesis are literally true, in respect either to the creation of man or to the prior creation of the natural world in which man lives. The Old Testament tales belong in the category of " myth," by which we mean (along with most contemporary theologians when they discuss the narratives) that these are stories that are told not about an event that happened in the distant past but about a fact that is true today; they are an imaginative way of expressing something about every human being and about the world in which he lives. And so far as the stories are concerned with man, they speak about the human condition as every man knows it when he understands himself: *de te fabula narratur,* as the Latin tag has it. Each one of us, every son of man, has a dependent existence; he is a created being, a " creature."

Therefore we must be clear that it is not a matter of God's literally breathing a spirit of life into man, who was literally fashioned as by some great artificer from the dust of the earth, and this far back in some remote past. Nor, to continue the Biblical account, is it a question of woman's being taken from man by the removal of a rib, again far back in that distant past. The Genesis account of the creation of woman is a way of asserting the " one flesh " relationship of the sexes, to which we shall return in a later chapter. And basic to the whole account is the patent fact that we did not make ourselves and that we do not explain ourselves. Here we have to do, not with some theory about a " first cause " to whom we owe our existence, but with the stark truth that always and everywhere, consciously or unconsciously, every man and woman owes existence to that which is not man or woman — we exist in an almost terrifying dependence upon something else or someone else than ourselves.

We depend, of course, upon our more immediate environment — family, friends, food, shelter, and the like. We depend also on a less immediate environment — history, the accumulated knowledge of the race, the created world itself in its many aspects. But, above all, we depend on the ultimate environment, on what religion calls God,

the Reality who is the final dependability, the enduring
" strength of all creation," the determiner of all destiny,
the perfect excellence, the most real of beings, and the
supreme goodness. The psalmist has a verse that puts it
inclusively: " It is he that hath made us, and not we ourselves."

We are creatures and we share with our fellowmen in
that creaturehood, that dependence. To pretend that we
are *in*dependent and *self*-explanatory is both vain and
stupid. Never has this been stated with greater power than
in some lines from Ezra Pound's *Pisan Cantos:*

> The ant's a centaur in his dragon world.
> Pull down thy vanity, it is not man
> Made courage, or made order, or made grace.
>   Pull down thy vanity, I say pull down.
> Learn of the green world what can be thy place
> In scaled invention or true artistry,
>   Pull down thy vanity. Paquin pull down!
> The green casque has outdone your eloquence.
>   Master thyself, then others shall thee bear . . .
>   Pull down thy vanity,
> Thou art a beaten dog beneath the hail,
> A swollen magpie in a fitful sun,
>   Half black, half white,
> Nor knowst thou wing from tail.
> Pull down thy vanity. How mean thy hates
> Fostered in falsity. Pull down thy vanity
> Rathe to destroy, niggard in charity,
> Pull down thy vanity,
>   I say pull down.[1]

The root of man's trouble, as we shall see in more detail
as we go farther in our description of human nature, is
precisely in this attempt which he makes to be *in*dependent.
The traditional word to define such an attempt and the

attitude that is associated with it is " pride." In our vain desire to run the world, in our pretense that we do run it, and in our efforts to run it, we manifest the pride which is our downfall. We fondly claim to be other than we are; we seek to evade, by our willful choice, the truth that we are creatures, dependent beings. This leads to an over-reaching of ourselves. We destroy our true humanity when we think of ourselves as " the hub of the universe." This is committing what Bertrand Russell once called an act of " cosmic impiety." And even for the man who does not acknowledge the existence of God, this impiety is fatal; for the consequence of it, in act, is that we see everything out of proper proportion and hence cannot act wisely and well. So we act inhumanly. Not only is it the case that by claiming what is not ours to claim, we make ourselves look absurd; more seriously, we then behave in such a fashion that we involve ourselves in fatal pretentions to self-assertion and the ironic result is that we really deny ourselves.

The opposite of pride is a genuine humility, which is nothing else than a sense of humor about ourselves, enabling us to understand and accept frankly and fully our many immediate dependences and in some fashion, however disguised it may be, our ultimate dependence. It is indeed " *he* that hath made us, and not we ourselves "; the honest man and the humble man has always known that something like this was the truth about him and he has never forgotten " his place " in the scheme of things. Our modern artificial life in great urban centers may hide the truth from our eyes; we may look at what *we* have made and worship ourselves as the maker of it — as someone has put it, whereas the firmament of heaven used to put us where we belong, neon lights in a city square tend to make us proud of our own doings. But the end product is always the same; we cannot avoid our dependence. And of this the fact of our death, to which we must come whether we will or not, is a dreadfully vivid reminder. Perhaps this is why we so much like to cover up the fact of death, with all the cheap art of the contemporary " mortician " and the inane euphemisms about " passing on " or " falling asleep " instead of the frank admission that we *die*. But however that may be, the fact is that we are inescapably dependent; and one of the keys to a truly healthful, rightly adjusted human existence is the recognition and acceptance of the fact.

But we must go on to the second statement in our schema: man is a creature, a dependent being, *with a purpose*. For the Christian, this truth about man means that he is made in " the image of God " and that he is intended to reach his fulfillment, to come to his full selfhood, by fellowship with God. Here there are several important things to say.

First of all, to speak in this fashion is to make clear that man is not only a dependent being but also a being who in that very dependence has a capacity for fulfillment. One might describe man as we find him and know him in ourselves as an *unfulfilled capacity*. There is a prospective quality about human life — a going on, a moving ahead, a " more " to be grasped and possessed. Some of our recent psychological writing has expressed this by speaking of man as a *dynamic* personality. He has a drive toward that which will give him further, and greater, self-realization.

In the Christian context, all this was said long ago by Augustine, in a famous sentence on the first page of his *Confessions*. In that " Grateful Witness " (which is probably the best translation of the title of his autobiographical

outpouring which we call the *Confessions*), Augustine
addresses God in these well-known words: *Tu fecisti nos ad
te, Domine, et inquietum est cor nostrum, donec requiescat
in te.* I give the Latin here because I wish to correct the
usual mistranslation of Augustine's words. Commonly we
find them put into the following English sentence: " Thou
hast made us for thyself, O Lord, and our heart is restless
until it rest in thee." But the Latin does not mean just
that. As any classicist knows, the force of the Latin preposi-
tion *ad* is movement, movement in a given direction which
is indicated by the accusative noun that follows the preposi-
tion. So with *ad te;* it means not " for thyself " but " toward thee "; it has a dynamic quality.

What Augustine is saying is that we men, by very reason
of our creaturely status, are made in such wise that we
necessarily move on toward some fulfillment; and he is
saying, further, that because every man is a creature made
by God, dependent ultimately upon God, explained only
by God, this drive toward fulfillment which is implanted
in him can be satisfied, finally, only in God who is his
enduring ultimate environment and his creator. God is
the supreme and final " end " of man's being. Hence, true
fulfillment, the fulfillment that alone will entirely satisfy
man's deepest yearnings, can be found only in God himself
and in no other. Without such fulfillment, Augustine goes
on to tell us, " our hearts are restless " — unquiet.
Augustine's *inquietum* is a very happy word for use at this
point. It expresses in precise Latin exactly what the modern
existentialist analysis of man in his actual given situation
regularly speaks of as his abiding " anxiety." When Søren
Kierkegaard used the term *Angst* as part of his basic definition of man's situation, he was describing the deeply rooted
inquietude, restlessness, dis-ease, which is so much a part

of the lot of every one of us in whatever age of the world's history we may be living, as we seek for fulfillment in that which does not finally satisfy. Man *is* this way.

But why is this so? It is because man is a creature who is made for fulfillment, yet in present fact is not fulfilled. Unless he moves toward that fulfillment — that realization of his potentiality — he is less than a true man; he is indeed only a somewhat sophisticated simian. And unless his drive for fulfillment is ultimately toward God, and not toward some other and lesser " end," his restlessness reflects his serious, sometimes his terrifying, falling short of that goal for which he has come into existence. Nothing less than God himself will *really* do. Ersatz fulfillments leave man with dust and ashes in his mouth. Francis Thompson wrote *The Hound of Heaven,* a poem often dismissed nowadays as flamboyant and exotic, to say just this. Whatever the merits of the poem may be as English verse, there have been few more eloquent or sustained statements of the truth that " naught satisfieth " man which is not leading him toward his final fulfillment in God. Thompson puts this in what might be described as " reverse terms "; that is, he portrays man as fleeing down " labyrinthine ways " to avoid that which alone can give him the rest that he needs and shows that even in his very running away from it he is really seeking it. All this is a way of saying that the drive in man is finally a drive toward God and that God is being sought even in ways that apparently deny his existence.

But it would be quite wrong to think that such fulfillment in God necessarily involves the acceptance of the conceptual pattern of some traditional theology. It can be, and probably often is, the case that in a given individual's reaction from some such scheme (imposed upon him in youth as an artificial set of beliefs with little or no vitality in them for the person upon whom they are forced) he is doing the precise opposite of running away from God; he may be, and often is, seeking a Reality behind and beyond the scheme he was taught — he is looking for, even being grasped by, what Paul Tillich has called " the God beyond theism " — although we must be careful that we understand by " theism " in this context not the Biblical picture of the dynamic God of nature and history but a god (with lower-case *g*) who is set alongside other equally real existents and hence is only another " being " among the many that man meets. Not only is true fulfillment of self entirely possible in the absence of any given theological description of God, although in the long run such may be required; it is possible even in the absence of *any* explicit theology. Furthermore, it is possible even to one who does not subscribe to the *concept* of God at all. For God is much more than a concept; he is a Reality — the ultimate dependability in things, the ground of all existence, the determiner of all destiny — and recognition of him as such may be conceptually very vague indeed. There *is* this Reality which in fact does fulfill human life, whatever may be the *name,* or *lack of name,* that men use in speaking of it.

Theology and theologies are at best feeble human attempts to explain, to expound, to explicate, what it means to be found of this Reality; but God is not confined, in his action in the world or in his attraction of his human creatures to himself, to any scheme of human thought. Neither is he operative only among those who call him, so to say, by his " proper name."

I once had a friend whose life seemed completely empty. He was restless, wearied, unquiet, in the depths of his being; there was a vacuum there which he could not fill. Superficially he seemed cheerful enough and he was certainly very successful in the eyes of the world. But he was a " hollow man," as Mr. Eliot has so well called this condition. Only when he began to develop a deep interest in — of all things! — the various interpretations of *Hamlet* which were then current did he begin to acquire a certain integration of life. Here was something that supplied him with an " end " that helped toward the fulfillment that hitherto he had not known. If he had not died in the Normandy invasion, I believe that this experience of his, found in his deep concern for interpretations of *Hamlet,* would have led him deeper and deeper until at length he would have discovered (especially if some of us who were his friends had been wise enough to give him understanding and assistance) that the Reality whom men have called God was in very truth drawing him to fulfillment in precisely this way — and eventually, perhaps, he could have been brought to a conscious recognition that it was God who all along had been at work in him.

I trust that this illustration does not seem ridiculous. If it does, it is only because I have put it badly; for there can be no doubt that what I have been describing was a wonderful, enriching, and fulfilling experience for my friend. Here was a man who had given up as silly and incredible the beliefs he had learned in childhood in a fairly strict family; his life had become a " wasteland " where nothing grew; it was " dust and ashes." And then, in some strange fashion, the supreme Reality who is the final dependability in things gave my friend the beginnings of an authentic life (to use Heidegger's word) , by working upon him and in him under this extraordinary incognito of interpretations of the great Shakespearean tragedy. Whatever tends to true fulfillment, whatever brings a man together through some mastering concern that takes possession of him, is the work of God; it is a place and a point where God's action is expressed and where something of his nature becomes transparent.

What has just been said raises all sorts of questions. The most serious of them is to what degree interests and concerns that seem doubtfully good, by any sound moral standard, or perhaps positively evil (if that is not a contradiction in terms), can serve as agencies of God for bringing men to fulfillment in him. At the moment one can say only that even the " idols " point in two directions. They point toward the God who is alone true fulfillment, and hence they are agencies of his working; and they point away from him toward lesser or even evil ways of obtaining ersatz fulfillment, and hence they are " of the devil " — in the last resort they are demonic or form-destroying agencies. Of this, more will be said at a later stage. But at this point, our only concern is to insist that almost any area of human life, almost any experience of men, can be used by God as an incognito for his fulfilling activity in men. And this must be added: for Christian faith the total life, death, risen life, and abiding power of one Man, Jesus of Nazareth — once that totality has been interpreted and understood, grasped and experienced, as the Christ of God — is the place where the supreme fulfillment of man is made possible *and* made actual. More than that, it is the place where such fulfillment is available for any man who will commit himself unreservedly to that One. This is why Jesus Christ is called the *kairos,* himself the fulfillment of time and the place of fulfillment in history, by such contemporary theologians as Paul Tillich — who perhaps more than any other in our day has seen the importance of what I have

just now called the incognitos of God and also of the necessity for a place of supreme and definitive fulfillment such
as Christian faith declares is discovered to us in Jesus
Christ. Jesus Christ is then for Christians the decisive moment in our human history, the moment in which precisely such rich fulfillment is available for men if they
let him grasp them and hold them in his grip. But we need
also to recognize that this claim of faith can only be validated if it is seen in a context such as that which I have
been describing.

Man is an unfulfilled capacity. That is the way he is
made; that is the secret of his creaturehood. He seeks all
sorts of roads to such fulfillment. Many of them are good
so far as they go; some of them are reflections of the vanity
or pride that besets man when he fails to remember that
he is a dependent being, a creature. But the basic truth
about him is that without fulfillment, or the drive toward
it, man is not completely man. He is at best but a potentiality, not an actuality, as man.

In concluding this chapter, I wish to link all that has
been said so far with the Christian affirmation that man is
" made in the image of God." That phrase means much
more than mere reflection as in a mirror. It means also,
and chiefly, the active and energizing capacity possessed by
man — or better, given to man — to live humanly, with
integrity, as a " created second " of the God who made him.
Now the distinctive affirmation of Christian faith is that in
Jesus Christ we have what Paul once called " the express
image of God." In him, manhood is truly fulfilled; he is
God's " idea " of what man is; he is the manifestation in
concrete human life of God's intention in creating the dependent being man; he is " what God is up to " in respect
to manhood. But if Christ is this, he is this only because in

him there is made actual, real, complete, vivid, and clear what is potential although unrealized and unaccomplished in every one of us men. He is the Truth about us, placarded on the pages of history in a genuinely human life about which we can read in a book called the New Testament.

But there is yet more to be said. For such making actual, such realizing, such completing, such bringing into vivid and clear focus, is not something which was or could be achieved by human effort and by that alone. Rather, it was and must be something that was " determined, dared, and done " (as Christopher Smart phrased it in his *Song of David*) by God himself. Certainly human effort was required; the Gospel narratives make it entirely clear that the manhood of Jesus is genuine manhood such as we know in ourselves. But the whole " act " of the manhood, the totality of the life of the Christ, is in its deepest signification *God's* act for man's wholeness, health, integration, fulfillment, " salvation ": it is what *God* did in true human life to the end that the rest of us could have these things. If the Christian claim that in the filial obedience of Christ we see the goal of human endeavor is true at all, it can be true only on those terms.

In his great book *Adventures of Ideas,* Prof. Alfred North Whitehead wrote as follows: " The essence of Christianity is the appeal to the life of Christ as a revelation of the nature of God and of his agency in the world. The record is fragmentary, inconsistent, and uncertain. It is not necessary for me to express any opinion as to the proper reconstruction of the most likely tale of historic fact. Such a procedure would be useless, without value, and entirely out of place in this book. But there can be no doubt as to what elements in the record have evoked a response from all that is best in human nature. The Mother, the Child, and the bare manger; the lowly man, homeless and self-forgetful, with his message of peace, love, and sympathy; the suffering, the agony, the tender words as life ebbed, the final despair; and the whole with the authority of supreme victory." [2] In this total human life, as Professor Whitehead goes on to say in his very next paragraph, there is the " revelation in act " of what otherwise and hitherto had been " divined in theory."

Now if all this be true, or if we can accept it at least tentatively as worthy of our most serious consideration, the way is prepared for something like the traditional Christian assertions about Jesus Christ. God so energized in this life, in this life which he himself had purposed and intended should be lived among us — creedally expressed in the words " conceived by the Holy Ghost, born of the Virgin Mary," however legendary the narrative of the Nativity may be — that those upon whom it first made, and those upon whom it still makes, its stupendous impact have been obliged to say that here, as nowhere else, God wrought in man, God lived in man, God was present in man. That is what the church means, deep underneath all its formulas and theologizing, when it talks of " the divinity of Jesus Christ."

When the Christian faith in Jesus Christ is set in this context, with full recognition of man as dependent and unfulfilled yet seeking genuine realization of his potentialities and able to find this only in relationship with the God upon whom ultimately he depends, that faith is far from being a teeny-weeny thing that hardly merits the attention of thoughtful and intelligent people. On the contrary, it has much to tell us about ourselves, much to say about our real problems as human beings, and much to offer in providing us with the answer to the question that sooner or later we all must ask: Who am I and what am I doing here in this world?

3

Man in Community and Man as Amphibian

Everyone is familiar these days with the idea of " community." We all know that no man lives unto himself. One of the best-known novels of this generation is Ernest Hemingway's *For Whom the Bell Tolls*,[3] the title of which is taken from a paragraph in a sermon by John Donne, the great Dean of St. Paul's in London. In this sermon Donne said that " no man is an Iland intire of it selfe," for he belongs to the great " Continent," so that we need not ask, " when the bell tolls a death," for whom it tolls. It tolls for each one of us, since we are part and parcel of the existence of every man who has ever lived, who now lives, or who ever will live. We are bound together in the common life of mankind. We are knit one with another " in the bundle of life," as the Old Testament puts it, and we can neither evade nor deny this fact about ourselves, try we ever so hard to live in arrogant individualism.

Hence, in speaking about man as created for community with others there is nothing new or surprising. What *is* new and surprising is the claim that so many make to self-contained lives. The pretense to " rugged individualism " which such persons seem to think establishes them as men is an astounding novelty in the history of the race, although many historical precedents are erroneously adduced for it.

The fact is, of course, that in those ages when our race has lived most deeply and genuinely, there has been a glad acceptance of our historical heritage, our social belonging, and our communal existence. The comparatively modern view of man which speaks of him in isolationist terms lacks depth because it lacks the awareness so keenly felt by our ancestors of the rich quality of corporate life, the sense of " tradition," and the acceptance of the fact of man's sociality.

The Christian understanding of human nature has always included this awareness. In its insistence that man is made for community it has meant much more than that he is part of a contemporary social group; it has meant that he belongs also to the whole past from which he has come, in all its variety, and the future which is before him, with all its mystery. Perhaps this awareness explains why the Christian church has seemed so committed in the educational institutions over which it has exercised control to " the humanities," seeing in such studies a means for developing the recognition in the group that they do indeed belong to a great historical community and plunging them back into the cultural heritage which is theirs, in the conviction that only in this fashion can they be alert to the contemporary situation and open to the future, whatever it may hold in store for them. But there is more than this involved in our community-belonging. The Christian faith has sought to make clear that if we are to achieve the fulfillment which comes from fellowship with God, we can do this only with the whole community of our brother men. We are not " windowless monads," in Leibniz's phrase; we are open to others and live in them as they live in us. And our fellowship with God is fully realized only when it is " in richest commonalty spread."

This fact establishes also the necessity for a social embodiment of religious faith. The life of man with God, and indeed the life of man as such, requires for its richest appropriation some institutional expression, some community of belief and worship and discipleship, which will give it a proper setting and enhance the experience of each participant. We need to remember, with Prof. R. H. Tawney, that the man who seeks for God entirely alone is " likely to find not God but the devil " and to discover that the devil " bears a surprising resemblance " to his own countenance. The truth is that the man who attempts to live religiously in isolation from his fellows is almost certainly bound to have a distorted picture of God, just as the man who attempts to live in a similar isolation in what we often call " secular ways " will almost certainly twist and warp his own personality and will have a peculiarly distorted picture of what proper human existence is really like. We need our fellows; and we need not only those who are with us today but also those who have walked this earth before us and can tell us what they have found. We need to have our little idiosyncrasies smoothed down by the wisdom of the ages and our favorite quirks balanced by the total encounter of mankind with life as it has been known and as it still is known. Religiously, above all, we need to have our special prejudices and our individualistic notions corrected, and our feeble insight and appreciation strengthened, by sharing with others of our race in the fullness of their experience of the divine Reality we name God.

Nowhere, perhaps, is this willingness to share more desperately needed than among the sophisticated and intellectually alert men and women of our own day. All too easily such persons fall victim, especially when they become interested in religious matters, to a kind of " God and myself " complex, in which (along with thinkers like Aldous Huxley) they eschew the social embodiments of faith and seek for a private mysticism that will undercut these expressions of religious life. Such persons are very ready to assume that by withdrawal from established religious communities they can enter upon a strictly " personal " relationship with God. But the fact is that to be a person *means* to be open and to share; and the retreat from the communal expression of religion is usually an escapism that is utterly unrealistic and likely to be utterly sterile. A mysticism that denies our human situation and sends us " alone to the Alone " is very frequently nothing but self-deception and illusion. For it is in the actual concrete circumstances of man's communal existence, as he " puts up " with the institutionalism which all historically vital religions have involved, that he can best and most surely find the divine Reality in fellowship with whom he can be fulfilled as a man.

Closely associated with this acceptance of the communal quality of human life is the awareness that each of us is a soul-body unity. This is the fourth constituent in a soundly human, and in a Christian, view of our nature as men.

Those who dislike communal life and above all disdain communal religion often have an equally deep distrust of man's bodily conditioning; they wish to be altogether " spiritual." They would flee from embodiedness in every form and would try to live as angels — who by definition of classical theology are intelligences without bodies. Of course there are those who take the opposite path. These think that life in the body is sufficient; and hence they succumb to the confusion that life *in* the body means life simply *as* a body; they seek to live as if they were animals, although animals of a sophisticated sort. But the truth is that we are all of us, as we know when we are honest in our self-appraisal, body-soul unities; we are embodied beings. There can be no getting away from this fact by attempts to fly into some cloud-cuckoo-land of " pure spirit," on the one hand, or by descents into the barnyard of sheer animality, on the other.

In the following pages we shall endeavor to develop this double theme of embodiedness — our corporate belonging and our corporeal existence, for perhaps nowhere else is the truth about men so badly misunderstood and the Christian interpretation of human existence so erroneously taught even in quite respectably Christian circles. As the result of our discussion we shall see how important it is to recognize that human nature is not only social in its deepest significance but is also a rich organic whole in which both body and soul are involved. And we shall come to a definition of man as a spiritual-social-physical organism, for whom spiritual aspirations and apprehensions, seeking for true fulfillment and genuine self-realization, are bound up together with social appurtenance and bodily existence.

Many of us still feel that Baron Friedrich von Hügel was the wisest, the most balanced, and in general the most profound writer on religious subjects in this century. And in considering the nature of man, we can turn to von Hügel and read: " We nowhere find, as a constituent of our human life and nature (except we ourselves make abstractions) , ' pure spirit,' or ' pure body,' or a ' purely ' spiritual or a ' purely ' bodily act. But everywhere we only find spirit awakened by, and in its turn awakening, checking, impelling, spiritualising body; and body furnishing such awakening, material friction, medium of expression and of appeal, yet also obstruction and deflection, to spirit." [4]

Nor does von Hügel speak alone in this matter. The witnesses to the truth which he is affirming range from Aristotle through Thomas Aquinas to William James. Aristotle insists on a realistic theory of knowledge; St. Thomas declares that " nothing is in the mind which is not first in the senses "; and William James, in *Psychology*, speaks of " the correlation of brain-states with mind-states." [5] All bear out von Hügel's contention; to use the phrase employed by him and also on one occasion and in this same connection by Evelyn Underhill, man is an " amphibian."

Obviously man is an animal; and he is, in many respects, like other members of the animal kingdom. But he differs from the rest of the animals in his capacity for thought: he is possessed of a " rational nature." Yet he is " conditioned," as the psychologists would put it, by the observable fact that he must receive the material for his thinking, must indeed do his thinking, by means of bodily instruments, even if the supreme instrument be the highly intricate and complex human brain. This is not to equate thinking with certain convolutions of the gray cells in the brain; it is, as James said, to correlate them. It is not to say that the music played by the violin is nothing more than the catgut of which in fact the strings are made; rather, it is to say that no violin music is possible, so far as we are aware, without the instrumental employment of those strings.

Man's body, in truth, is an intricately developed means whereby he acts and wherein he acts. Man's body is also a means whereby he receives impressions and is able to know whatever it is that he does know. It is possible that there are other means of knowing — nonsensory means. But of these we have very little knowledge indeed; and it is not only wisdom but common sense that insists upon some kind of check, such as sensible perception provides, upon the too ready use by many writers of vague terms like " intuition."

The problem of the relation of the mind which knows to the body by which it knows is a very complicated one; it is not for us in this discussion to attempt to solve it. However, there can be no doubt about one thing: ordinary human experience makes the simple observation that the body is an inalienable and essential element in the functioning of the human personality, and that man himself, as an existing personality, is in the words of Francis Thompson the " wedding " of

> . . . two worlds immense
> Of spirit and of sense.

As far back as infancy, the "human animal" learns chiefly through his bodily experiences. Things, persons, happenings of one sort or another " bump " up against him. By responding to these insistent pressures and by relating them one to another in his total organism, he comes to that point of experience where it is possible for him to make some sort of " rational " account both of them and of life as he is obliged to live it. It is in, through, with, and under his physical experiences that his mental processes begin to operate, come to maturity, and start to react upon his bodily actions, so that the latter may express what initially they received, worked upon, ordered, and related when taken into the organism as impressions.

So it is that the body serves not only as the recipient of stimuli but also as the agent for reaction and for action. We emphasize the latter since it appears that some have felt that all men can do is to *react* to stimuli; whereas a consideration of the deliverances of our experience shows plainly, unless we are entirely misled by what we think we do, that we can initiate a series of events in the physical world, both in the world of our bodies and in the world that exists externally to us. The attempt to reduce all human behavior to a *merely* responsive movement, without any initiating capacity whatever, would make man but an automaton — a view that is logically self-condemned because it eviscerates truth of meaning and thus destroys the very hypothesis that it advocates. So we come to understand that the body is both the impressive and the expressive agent for the total human personality, while the " engineer " of the personality is the total rationality of man — his reason. In the famous Scholastic definition, man is called " an individual substance of a rational nature "; in another idiom, he has been described as the animal who thinks. And because he thinks, he is therefore *sui generis,* different from the other animals in whom thinking is not the specific quality.

But one important fact is often forgotten in this account of man as a rational being. That often forgotten fact is the place of the emotional life in his total pattern. While it is indeed true that man as man is a rational animal, and while it must be taken for granted — indeed, insisted upon — that he functions through his body when he functions at all, it is not so frequently recognized that part of man's functioning, and therefore an essential element in a correct understanding of what is involved in his rationality, is that side of him which responds to the external world or goes out to the external world in terms of " feeling tone." Men say, over and over again, as they respond to the pressures of experience, " I like it," " I dislike it," " I enjoy it," " I hate it." Here is a genuine part of human living, which we forget at our peril. Even more serious is the tendency to overlook the glandular, visceral, in brief, the organic, basis for this emotional life of man as well as for his rationality. It is as if man could somehow be seen as a mind inhabiting a body from which had been removed all that makes it warmly and distinctively a body. But this is not the fact which our simplest experiences of perception, not to mention our higher experiences of human fellowship, make plain to us. I can never dissociate myself, either as a body or as a thinking being, from the reality of my appreciating, depreciating, liking, disliking, desiring or not desiring. As a man, I am emotionally constituted.

Furthermore, as a man compounded of soul and body, each of us dwells in community. That is to say, our experiencing of life is socially prepared; that which we know is mediated to us, to a large degree, through our " contacts " with other men, and not least through our participation in the social tradition of which we are a part. It is impossible to envisage man without sociality. The " Good Man Friday " who lives alone, with never a human relationship, is not truly a man. However he may be regarded, he is surely not human in the deepest sense of the term, which means to be a member of, a sharer in, and a recipient of, life from, and a giver of life to, a community in which he takes his place.

The consequence of this " social conditionedness " of man is that he must not only express himself and also receive impressions through bodily media; he must also be dependent upon his social environment for his perceptions of fact and idea. He can no more get away from society than he can get out of his own skin. He may regard society as friendly to him or as alien to him; nevertheless, he depends upon it. He may dislike his life in community, or he may accept it gladly and freely; he cannot escape it. The institutions of human corporate existence are part of the total framework of life as we men must live it.

It is interesting and significant that as we speak of man's physical body as his *corporeal* nature, so we use the same

Latin root to describe his social appurtenance: we speak of man in his *corporate* nature. This is an indication, perhaps, that the race has understood that in a very real sense society is an extension of man's embodiedness. It is not at all an accident; it is part of man's being as the strange amphibian that he is.

Nothing has brought this so clearly home to us as the tremendous upsurge of racism and the emphasis on folk and state. J. W. Harvey, in an article in the English journal *Philosophy,* November, 1944, said that while the Nazi party philosophy had much that was vicious in it, it did at least recognize something that Western democracies have tended to forget in their emphasis on " individualism," [6] namely, that man as man is only fulfilled when he is in intimate, interpenetrating, and appreciative relationship with his fellows in a common social life. It is extraordinary that many are even now not able to see this truth when it is so strikingly, not to say stridently, thrust before their eyes precisely because its denial gave rise to so startling and shocking a perversion.

We may assume, then, that for any balanced view man is understood as a body-mind-society complex. But here another point needs attention, one that has also frequently been overlooked. In this picture of man as society-body-mind, the *prevenient* action — the initiating step in the rich interplay between mind, body, and society — comes from the outside. Man is a focus for influences and drives that play upon him; it has even been suggested that his development is like that of the eye — the rays of the sun beat down upon the organism, cause an irritation that in its turn undergoes considerable development, and presently the result is the emergence of the seeing agent of the organism. So, it has been urged, man is initially provoked into rationality, or his latent rationality is urged into activity, by the play of the external world upon him through his sensory apparatus. There is surely some truth in this theory, which (in our judgment) may be held without succumbing to blank materialism as so many thinkers have sought to prove. The important consideration for our discussion, however, is that the outside world is really *there,* independent of us and yet meeting us through our experience and making its inexorable demands upon us for adjustment to it.

Such a view is sheer common sense. It is only when sophisticated thinkers begin to work upon the deliverances of experience that they produce a complicated epistemology that would deny this view. But the strange thing is that the very thinkers who deny the view themselves live by it in their nonprofessional moments. The epistemological " idealist " is obliged to treat his wife, his child, his friends, his armchair, his lamb chop, his pencil, as something other than a construct of the mind; these things are *there,* and wisely or unwisely he trusts his sense experience when it tells him they are there. And he approaches the world through his body, even when he most minimizes that body and its place in the world.

Baron von Hügel once remarked that he kissed his baby because he loved it, while he loved it the more because he kissed it. So it is in all our knowledge, through all our life. We know one another because we see, hear, touch one another; while the very fact of our sensible understanding deepens the knowledge that it inaugurates. It is absurd to neglect this truth about ordinary human life; even in our most elevated and " spiritual " contacts, it is the *thereness* of the other, our perception of him through the senses, which makes the relationship possible and is the condition of the communion of soul with soul that delights us. So likewise with our experience of the world. Although our senses do err (and here surely the Scholastics were wrong), they also deliver to us what they apprehend to be *there*, what they feel or see or hear or smell or grasp in some over-all organic fashion. We can readily admit that our physical instrumentalities may not be adequate fully to receive or to express, yet they are essential for the expression of our-selves, as well as for the reception of " information " from outside us.

It is the fact that if we wish not merely to know about our world but also to " get ourselves across," we must em-ploy our bodies. Sometimes the denial of this bodily instru-mentality leads to absurd conclusions. It is as if one should say to his friend, " I like you so much that I won't clasp your hand," or to his wife, " I love you so dearly that I cannot kiss you." The unnaturalness and inhumanity of such actions would rightly condemn them — and that is the nub of the matter.

Thomas Aquinas has put the point well when he writes, in *Summa Theologica,* " By means of external signs, whether of words or deeds, the human mind is moved as regards apprehension and consequently also as regards the affections." He has put the other side of the matter, too, when he says, " It is connatural for us to proceed from the sensible to the intelligible," and therefore it is " befitting to man that he should employ sensible signs in order to signify anything, because he derives his knowledge from sensibles." [7]

We have come to see, then, that man is an amphibian being, with soul or mind penetrating body, or body at one with soul or mind: that is, he is a soul-body or body-mind organism living organically with society. His distinctive feature is his rationality; this marks him out from the other animals. But the fact that he is so endowed does not make it possible for him to slip out of his body, and think and act as if he were not possessed of one. " Angelism " is quite as serious an error as " animalism," which would treat man as if he were *nothing but* a body. The danger for religiously minded folk is that they tend to underestimate the bodily side of man, and sometimes appear even to wish that he were not in the body at all. This is the ancient heresy of Docetism, but it is not unknown today — not merely among Christian Scientists but among many Christians whose religion is so " spiritual " that it has no contact with the hard, rude, factual world in which bodies, dirt, and stuff are to be found.

The sound and Christian attitude is that so well expressed in a line by the late Percy Dearmer, when he speaks of " the wonder and weakness of flesh." It is a glorious thing, a " wonder," that the human body is here; yet there is a " weakness " about it, for not merely may it partially deceive us in its deliverances about the world, but it is also inadequate to express the " more " that is deep within man. Man's embodiedness is both his tragedy and his grandeur, but it is an inescapable fact. And in religion, as everywhere else in life, we do well to accept the facts humbly and gratefully.

As we have seen, the Christian faith has been extraordinarily insistent on all this. Despite much misunderstanding of its position, even by writers and thinkers who themselves were professed Christians, the mainstream of historical Christianity quite consistently has seen and emphasized these truths. It has declared that Jesus Christ himself has " come in the flesh." It has replaced the Greek conception of " immortality of the soul " by the apparently very difficult belief in the "resurrection of the body," or where a substitution of the latter for the former failed has qualified the meaning of "immortality of the soul," so that total personality, rather than some vague spiritual entity, has been implied. On the other hand, it has not thought for a moment that man's body is to be regarded as all there is to him, so that the body's immediate inclinations and desires, its biological drives and its achievement of physical satisfaction, may be given entirely free rein with no governance or control by his responsible use of reason. Neither has it thought that the fullest acceptance of man's sociality can deny or diminish the reality of his personal selfhood. It has believed that both the physical body and the social belonging of man are so much part of his total being that man can find true meaning for both only when they are related to personal and — if the word is used in its correct sense — spiritual aspirations and desires.

Thus the Christian faith has been concerned with man as he really is: an embodied being whose existence is in and with his fellowmen. In Biblical language, the Christian tradition has spoken of *sarx* — the reality of our historical, social, embodied existence. That is how we men live, with the capacity for relationship with God — which is what is meant when we are told that we have or that we are "spirits." This whole portrayal of man is a measure of the realism and accuracy of the Christian perspective.

To be thus embodied and to live thus in community carries the consequence that what we do "materially" and what we are "socially" have supreme importance in establishing what our human existence really is. What happens to us in these ways affects *us* in our manhood. Hence the whole social and physical character of human experience, with its extension in the houses in which we dwell, the surroundings in which we live, the kind of jobs which we have, the material conditions of our work, the structure of the society to which we belong, with the resultant economic and political and national and international situation, counts enormously in making us what we are. On the other hand, as we have just seen, we are unable to express ourselves, humanly speaking, in this world in which we are placed, without the use of our bodies and the social extension of our personality. These too are so much bound up with ourselves that even in the highest aesthetic, intellectual, moral, and religious activities we depend upon them to " get ourselves across."

I need not point out the close relationship all this bears to the new insight into the psychosomatic nature of illness and disease as well as to the cultural or social conditioning of true health and integration. It is becoming more and more evident that physical ills, neurotic and psychotic states so far as emotional and mental life are concerned, and religiously described facts of human experience like sin and guilt and like grace and salvation, are bound together in a remarkable way. So more and more we are coming to recognize that the cultural and social aspects of human sickness and of human health have a deep and inescapable relationship to religious adjustment and spiritual integrity. The Christian concern for man's body and his society are validated by scientific investigation and medical research.

Furthermore, the Christian insistence on the embodied and social nature of man has been so strong that it has been extended even beyond the grave. Some religious people still talk of a kind of natural immortality which they feel is proper to " the soul." But in the great tradition Christians (as I have pointed out) have affirmed in their creeds the

" resurrection of the body " — or better, perhaps, with the Nicene Creed in its correct translation, " resurrection from the dead." This affirmation has been seriously misunderstood and misinterpreted by literal-minded persons who have mistakenly assumed that it meant that the physics and chemistry, not to mention the biology, which are now ours will somehow be " raised " or " restored " in a definitely physical resurrection. So they have opposed cremation, for example. But as a matter of fact, informed Christians who understand the metaphorical nature of the language of religion and the way in which in the Scriptures profound and inescapable truths are affirmed in pictorial fashion take no such crude position. They have seen that the creedal assertion is a way of saying that as in this life we are embodied beings, living in social relationships, so in whatever life lies beyond this one, such embodiedness and sociality cannot be sloughed off or lost — if they were, it would no longer be *men* to whom eternal life was given.

Doubtless the mode of embodiment and the expression of sociality will be proper to that heavenly state which, Paul tells us, " flesh and blood cannot inherit." Resurrection means, as the paradoxical Pauline phrase " spiritual body " implies, a kind of existence appropriate to fulfilled fellowship with God in communion with our brethren — in " the communion of saints," in fact. This is the condition for self-expression and self-realization, as it is also the condition for the richest and deepest sharing of life. We cannot put this into neat logical concepts nor can we picture this state; but what we expect — look for, hope for, wait for, as the New Testament phrases it — is some form of personal existence, in and under God and in complete fellowship with him, which will provide genuine continuity for human personality and at the same time make possible genuine community with others.

A truer understanding of man, along such lines as those which we have here presented, may help to save us from falling into the error of treating men as if they were pale, disembodied, lonely creatures, lacking the richness and warmth which are so genuine and lovely a part of human experience in its deepest ranges. The implications of all this for Christianity are indeed profound. The strange and wonderful thing is that Christian faith — with its affirmations about the incarnation, or enmanment, of God in human life, its concept of the church as " the mystical body of Christ," its sacramental mode of worship, its social as well as its personal gospel, its insistence on resurrection — fits, as by divine intention, into the facts about man's nature which so-called secular inquiry has discovered. Perhaps one difficulty in our own day has been that we have overlooked some exceedingly important truths, both in secular wisdom and in Christian faith.

I. Note on " Spiritual Healing "

In view of the strong and repeated emphasis in these chapters on the psychosomatic nature of man, it may be well to append a few comments on the question of " spiritual healing," interest in which has greatly increased during the past few years — and not only among the sects that are avowedly based on this interest, like the so-called Christian Scientists, but also among many groups within the established Christian churches.

Much of the argument for " spiritual healing " has been based on the very point upon which we have been so emphatic — that man is neither soul nor mind alone, nor body alone, but an organism functioning in both psychological and physiological ways, and with a relationship to

God that effects still another way of functioning, namely, a spiritual way. Furthermore, the notion that " salvation " is closely related to, indeed, identical with, total personal " wholeness " or " health " would also seem to lend weight to the case for " spiritual healing." If it is true that man's spiritual condition is so intimately related to his psychological and physiological structure, and further, if it is true that God purposes " wholeness " or " health " for his human children, what more likely than that the " healing " of the spirit of man will result in the healing also of his mind, his emotions, and his physical body?

It seems to me, however, that the argument as commonly presented is so one-sided that it comes to a false conclusion. Once again we need to remember the old truth that the context in which a statement is made has its enormous effect on the truth of the content of the statement. It is indeed true that God wills wholeness for man, but this need not imply that the kind of wholeness which is willed is always and necessarily perfect physical health in the present world, and hence that illness, pain, and even death itself are utterly contrary to the divine purpose. We may argue, with better logic in view of the facts before us, that God's *ultimate* will for man is indeed total health of human personality; but it would be entirely within the range of possibility — and I myself believe that it is the case — that in the immediate world of our experience, illness, pain, and death are within the *permissive* will of God. That is, God has created and continues to create and sustain a world in which these things do in fact occur and in which, as and when they occur, they may be used by God for the attainment of the ultimate goal of a total personal health in which through illness and pain and death itself man in his organic richness (his total personality reconstituted at death through what we call "resurrection") may be brought to the divinely intended goal. Hence, although we cannot say that God wills *directly* that this or that person shall be ill, or suffer pain, or die, we can say that in this world, as we know it, the processes of nature and of human life work in such a fashion that human life does experience all of these; and therefore that in a profound, although certainly not in an obvious, sense, God's will is being done through these things.

In the second place, while cooperation between clergymen and medical men is not only desirable but essential, this should not be thought to mean that the clergyman is to take the place of the medical man, any more than the medical man is to assume the role of the clergyman. A proper understanding of the implications of man's psychosomatic nature should lead to a total attack upon man's illness and maladjustment. The medical man and the psychiatrist should work to bring about such health of the body, emotions, and mind as can be secured by the methods which are appropriate to their disciplines, while the clergyman should on his part seek to establish or deepen the relationship of the patient with God himself.

Two consequences would follow. First, since man is an organic unity, health of body may very often lead toward health of spirit — although this is by no means always the case and especially is it lacking when the attempt is to create a healthy physical and psychological life without regard for the fullness of relation to God, for in that situation a self-centered regard for physical and emotional health is all too likely to lead to pride and satisfaction. On the other hand, the development of a faithful and devout relationship with God may very often lead to better health in physical and emotional life, since the attitude of serenity and quiet trust in God can very well "overflow," so to

say, and have profound effects in the more strictly physiological and psychological functioning of man — although,
once again, we must recognize that there is no guarantee
that this will happen and we must acknowledge that often
the greatest saints have *not* been robust and healthy speci-
mens physiologically and psychologically.

The total health of the human personality, then, is not
something that we can assume will always and necessarily
be fully realized in the world of our present experience.
On the other hand, this should not for a moment deflect us
from making and supporting every effort to bring about,
through spiritual guidance and help, through psychological
assistance of various kinds, and through the labors of the
physician and surgeon, the best functioning that is possible
for each and every son of man at all levels of his personality.
That is a Christian and also a humane obligation. All I
am arguing is that we should not permit ourselves to fall
into the error of thinking that in the world as we now
know it and live in it, the final perfection of man is guar-
anteed to us — either by spiritual ministrations or by medical and psychiatric treatment. Nor does this create a
problem that better knowledge may solve; rather, in my
opinion, it is part of the mystery of human existence in its
historical setting in this natural order — a mystery to which
God alone knows the full answer, but also a mystery that
in Christian faith at any rate, is met by the affirmation that
for men " there is all this, and heaven too," or, in the words
of Mother Julian of Norwich, which we have quoted in the
main text of this book, " All shall be well, all manner of
thing shall be well."

II. Note on Pauline Terms

Since reference has been made in the text to Paul's use
of terms in describing the nature of man, it may be helpful

to add here a brief note on this point of New Testament usage.[8]

Whereas the Johannine literature seems to adopt a fairly simple practical dualism between " flesh," or the material and physical aspect of human nature, and " spirit," or the immaterial and (in the modern sense) spiritual aspect — a *practical* dualism which ought not to be taken as suggesting that the Johannine writer or writers subscribe to the radical dualism found in much of the thought of the Greco-Roman world — the Pauline literature has a much more complicated or complex view of man. This is not the place, nor is the writer competent, to provide a complete word study that would cover the entire field; it may be suggested that the following scheme seems to be in the mind of Paul and in those writers of New Testament works (e.g., Colossians and Ephesians) which are perhaps not by Paul himself but are certainly Pauline in general spirit and content.

Sōma (body) is regularly used to denote the material or physical side of human nature; it is a way of speaking of all that we should call man's physiological nature. *Sometimes* it has a wider meaning, for example, occasionally approximating *sarx,* and now and again denoting man's total being or self.

Sarx (flesh), which is often confused with *sōma* in discussion of Paul's thought, should in fact be quite carefully distinguished from it. *Sarx* refers to the total physical-societal-historical nature of man; it denotes the fact that each man is so situated that he lives in and exists within the context of a given determinate physical, social, and historical scene — he is an earthly creature whose existence is in *this* world and in *this* mode of existence. Since the situation in which man lives and hence the participation which obtains for man in his world is for Paul vitiated by sin, the word *sarx* can also on occasion mean the sinfulness of man's nature in its alienation from God and in its estrangement from the divine intention for it.

Psychē (soul) is used to indicate the fact that man is not only " of the dust " but is also an animate, living being; it is not to be confused with man's capacity for relationship with God, which has to do with his genuinely " spiritual " quality, but rather with his *life* as distinguishing him from the animals which do not possess a *psychē* or soul.

Nous (mind or reason) denotes the fact that man is not only a physiological creature, not only immersed in a historical situation that is integral to his nature, not only an animate or living being, but also a reasonable or rational being. Man's *nous* might be described as his intellectual or cognitive powers; but it is rather more than this, for it is also employed to make the point that man is capable of acting in accord with the *Logos* (although this is not a Pauline word; cf., however, the Romans passage about man's " reasonable service," where *logikos* has this other sense, Rom. 12:1), that is to say, with the principle of reason which is basic to his existence as made " in the image of God."

Pneuma (spirit) indicates that man, in addition to all the aspects of his nature and the capacities that are his, to which we have referred above, has also the capacity to be related to God who himself is " Spirit " (nonmaterial, yet related also to that which is not divine). It might perhaps be said that *penuma* has in Pauline thought this specific *relational* connotation; for Paul, man is, above all, " the child of God " and a potential " son of God," and this reality and potentiality are suggested in man's spiritual discernment which enables him to be in communion with his Creator. There is some variation in the way in which the term is employed, but generally the thought of Paul is that such a spiritual quality and capacity in man, however latent it may be in all men, requires for its quickening into effectual and patent reality an action on the part of God toward and in man. That action is the work of " the Spirit," whether of God or of Christ or *sans phrase,* whose economy seems to be (so far as man is concerned) precisely this awakening and developing, as by a gift, of the possibility of man's responsive communion with God.

As I have said, the usage in the Pauline literature is not always entirely consistent, and there are a number of problematic passages where the meaning is not at all clear even to careful students. However, the scheme that has just been outlined will serve for a general picture, and we may summarize it as follows: for Paul, man is a creature of God, with a physical nature and yet with a rational capacity; he is involved in the given material, social, and historical situation which belongs to his mortality as such a creature in this world, yet he has the ability to act, to greater or lesser degree, in accordance with his rational powers; on the other hand, because the situation in which he finds himself and with which he is integrally united is a sinful one, he is alienated from God and unable to express his latent openness for communion with God; but by the action of God upon him, chiefly in Jesus Christ and the response made in faith to that Lord, the " spirit " in him is quickened by " the Spirit " sent or given by God; when this occurs, man is conformed to the Image of God, which is Jesus Christ (the full or perfected man who is God's expressive act), and hence is brought to the state where the image in which he is made is reflected in the total personality that is his.

4

Embodied Man and Sacramental Life and Worship

The important truths, both Christian and secular, to which we have referred in the last chapter, have to do with the fact that as men we live in and by our corporeal bodies and by necessity belong to the corporate body, and the equally patent fact, known in Christian faith, that God has created us as dependent creatures, made for him in community with others, and living the inescapably double life of " spirit and sense." It is not surprising, therefore, that historically the life of the Christian church has found its center in worship of a sacramental character. And so we come to the next (fifth) point in our developing description of man: it is natural that his relationship with God shall be sustained by sacramental means.

Indeed, we might say that it is not only natural but inevitable for man, constituted as he is, to worship the divine Reality he calls God by following along the lines prescribed by his embodiedness and his participation with his fellows in social relationships. Whether it be through the sacramental medium of the Word preached to a congregation by human lips and heard by human ears, or through the sacramental rite of the Word enacted in the Eucharistic action in which bread and wine are set apart and received by the worshipers in a corporate action, fellowship with God is appropriately established and the relationship sustained with due dependence on man's materiality and sociality. It is of course true that the corporate worship of the institution is complemented by the personal devotion of each believer; but it is equally true that personal devotion without social expression is felt to lack the full-orbed quality of Christian worship as the Christian ages have understood its meaning.

We can speak of " sacrament " in a general and in a special sense. In the special (and specifically Christian) sense the reference is, of course, to Holy Baptism and Holy Communion. These (and other sacramental rites, whatever they may be) have been given classic definition in a sentence of Hugh of St. Victor: " a corporeal or material element offered to the senses, which from likeness represents, from institution signifies, and from consecration contains, some invisible and spiritual grace." [9] I should prefer to alter some few of the words in that definition, changing " element " to " action " and " contains " to " conveys," in order to establish the dynamic nature of the sacramental reality and to give proper weight to Dr. Hastings Rashdall's sound principle that " a thing is where it acts." [10] But a wider definition of sacrament, which permits of application to more than Holy Baptism and Holy Communion, is that of Augustine, who tells us that a sacrament is *signum sacrum* or *signum rei sacrae* (a sacred sign or the sign of a holy reality) .[11] And the Catechism of *The Book of Common Prayer* gives a definition that, if one comes to a stop with the opening phrases, has a similar wider application: " an outward and visible sign of an inward and spiritual grace." So soon as we continue with the Prayer Book definition, of course, with its reference to ordination by Christ and the purposes for which the sacrament exists, we find ourselves in the realm of the specifically Christian sacramental theology.

Contrary to the usual practice, I wish to begin our consideration with sacrament in its broader meaning, in its natural sense, in its widest import. Doubtless it is true that sacramentalism in this more universal significance is the consequence of deepening experience of the specific sacraments of the Christian tradition; yet I am more and more convinced that a sound understanding of the whole matter of sacramental worship and of the importance of the particular sacraments of the Christian church, as they illuminate our view of man and his world, must begin with the recognition that this worship and these sacraments are from one point of view (and that a profoundly important one) special instances or vivid illustrations of a general sacramental character which is proper to the whole created order. Grace, we are told by Thomas Aquinas,[12] perfects nature. It does not destroy the naturally good creation of God but brings that creation to its intended goal and its proper fruition. In a similar fashion the special sacraments of the church are not contradictory to or a denial of the natural sacramental order of creation; on the contrary, they crown and complete that order by its full and intentional infusion by, informing with, divine grace in a particularly and peculiarly intensive and distinctive way.

Man himself is a sacramental being. Francis Thompson has expressed this idea poetically:

> In this narrow bed,
> Spirit and sense are wed.

Thus he speaks of human personality. The poet Edmund Spenser raised the question whether body helps soul more than soul helps body. And as we have seen in the preceding chapter, it is a fact of common experience that our materiality or corporeality is the expressive medium for our personal *selves*. Our bodies are the vehicle by which we act, in which we more than dwell, for in them we *are* and through them we " get ourselves across." Indeed, we may say quite simply: no body — no man. A spiritualism that would deny man's genuine " body-ness " is nonsense; for at the same time it denies the truths of his existence which are most directly familiar to him. We have already pointed out that even in thought itself — the act which, as Aquinas tells us, is proper to man as rational being, and hence distinguishes him from mere animals — the process, although doubtless mental and spiritual, is carried on upon the basis of convolutions of some millions of gray cells in the brain. Man is no angel, despite some of our modern " idealists "; neither is he mere animal, as contemporary " naturalists " (in the cheaper use of that word) would suggest. He is mind-body, body-mind, amphibian in his constitution.

Secondly, the entire world of our experience is sacramental. That is to say, in that world, values, ideals, purposes, spiritual realities of all sorts, are expressed and operative only in, through, and under material or corporeal realities. No one has ever seen goodness; we have only seen good actions, good deeds, goodness bodied forth to us through the visibly real. No one has ever seen beauty; we have only known beautiful landscapes, beautiful objects or forms, beautiful faces or phrases. No one has ever seen or known truth; we have acquaintance only with true propositions or statements. No one has ever known love, in its unmediated essence; we have but glimpsed it incarnate in persons or works. So it is with all the other values or (as we say) spiritual realities. They are sacramentally known to us; and they are known to us in no other fashion. And when we find God, it is most securely and certainly in this manner. St. Thomas says that through signs that can be perceived by the senses the mind is stimulated in its movement toward God; [13] and it is part of the wisdom of historical Christianity that it has tended to be suspicious of, though never to deny the possibility of, religious experience and mysticism when these are not regulated and controlled by the sheer common sense of the ordinary man's mode of perception and his normal way of reaching divine Reality.

The phrase from St. Thomas leads us to a third general truth which is frequently neglected. We have cited Baron von Hügel's remark that he kissed his child, not only *because* he loved it, but also in order that he might love it *more*. In other words, the experience of men goes to show that physical contacts, material realities, things done in the realm of the corporeal, tangible, visible, and sensible, are the most effective way in which states of mind, attitudes, beliefs, and certainties of many sorts may be stimulated, may even be inaugurated, as well as deepened and enriched. In marriage, for example, the physical relationship of sexual intercourse does not merely express a spiritual love between man and wife; the physical act deepens and makes more real that love. So we might run through the whole range of human activities and of human experience of the physical world — one's potential awareness of values such as goodness and beauty, for example, is stimulated into actuality by the impact of good or beautiful objects and actions; and in religion, the material world both speaks for and conveys effectively the presence and the action of God to the reverent and humble mind.

Finally, when the divine Being himself made his highest and deepest declaration of himself to men and entered into the closest and most intimate possible relationship with them, he was obliged — yes, we ought to be prepared to put it as strongly as that — to become incarnate, to unite himself with One of our own kind, who was held a baby in the arms of the blessed mother, walked and lived with us as a man, died and rose again as a man — for only so could he really come to us; only so could we receive him eventually as Spirit, by the Holy Spirit, precisely because he had been among us and with us in our own human terms. The incarnation as a historic moment in the relationship between God and man is therefore both part of, and the quickening action in, an incarnational universe, a sacramental world, in which man always lives by sacraments.

Every good reality in its degree is a " sacred sign," or a " sign of a sacred reality." But not each in the same degree. This is a world that in our experience is multiform, various, richly graded with all manner of difference and distinction. The star says something that the flower petal cannot say; the delicate coloring of a cloud is symbolic and sacramental in a different sense from a man's action. Some things are very limited in their expressive power as also in their evocative potentialities, while others have much greater capacity for such expression and evocation — almost to the point (but never quite to it, even in the humanity of our Lord) of being infinite in their evocative and expressive range. Furthermore, there is the fact of sin — a disagreeable fact to contemplate, but a real one nevertheless. There is evil in the world. Evil means, in another way of phrasing it, that there is in the created world disorderliness, maladjustment of vehicle to purpose, disproportion in the arrangements of the relatively good realities which makes them unworthy and misleading; while sin means that there is a dis-ease in man which can, and observably does, lead to a state of alienation from his true end and hence to actual sinning, because it involves an inordinate or disproportionate employment of his desire toward ends that are not finally good. Thus it is that there can be a perversion of the *sacra signa* into *signa inordinationis* (signs of disorder) and even into *signa inordinata* (disordered signs). But on the other hand, there are the high points in creation where the deepest significance is given to the whole system of symbolic realities. The " great moments " of life, the supremely meaningful actions, the utterly beautiful forms, the contacts that most intimately relate us to others or to God — here are criteria for the whole system because here is the open coronation of that which in the less significant events and things and contacts has been secretly initiated.

Let us now turn from this general presentation of the natural sacramentalism of life and the world to the area in which such intensifications of the sacramental occur that we may properly speak of them as very specially related to God's way and work for men. That area or " field " is the church understood as the body of Christ. First it is essential to recognize that this term " the body of Christ " is an apt description of the church. Not only because Paul frequently employed it, but also because it is the best way of picturing the relation of the church to Christ, the term " body " has been applied to the fellowship of Christian believers. For as in his personal humanity our Lord had for his self-expression and for his evocative action among men a corporeal body that was the perfected vehicle for his divine purpose, so in the society which came into being through his action and exists to convey his Person and gospel through the centuries, he has a " body " — but now a social body — which is the vehicle for his purpose and which in its members is on the way to increasing perfection as it more nearly realizes its true nature as his vehicle. Despite the sin, the error, and the weakness of its human members, the church is the " mystical body of Christ," the sacramental agency for the unseen yet present and active Lord. The term " body of Christ " as applied to the church must indeed be taken as a metaphor, but taken *very seriously* as a metaphor, with the understanding that it is the most adequate symbol for the truth about the church. Hence the body of Christ is the continuing organic expression of the life of him in whom God lived most richly among us; it is informed by life-in-love because it is itself life-in-union; its head is the everlasting Christ and its secret life is the Holy Spirit who is the charity of God; its purpose is the incorporation of all men into Christ; its end is the return of men with the entire creation to God, so that he may be sacramentally expressed and active throughout that entire creation by free and glad surrender to his purpose, until all shall find itself in him.

Such a picture of the church rules out completely any mechanical or legal view of its nature. One need not agree with the extreme denial of all " law " in the church, to which Dr. Walter Lowrie,[14] for example, found himself led many years ago, but one must at least agree with the insistence of Dr. Lowrie and others that in the church organizational factors are secondary to the vital, dynamic, and organic. Nor does this mean that there are no established ways of functioning that are significant in and important to the church, any more than recognition of the human body as a totally functioning organism implies that it possesses no salutary and necessary agencies or ways of normal healthy functioning. For myself, for instance, I should insist that the ministry of the church is a mode of functioning which is intrinsic to the life of the body. But that could not imply that this ministry is detached, automatic, external succession. The ministry must itself be a sacrament of a sacred thing, namely, of the historic continuity and the genuine self-identity of the church as body of Christ. It is important to say, thus plainly and flatly, that the sacramental life of the church is a " system " only in the sense in which the human organism has certain ways of functioning which are essential to its true health, true persistence, true identity. The sacraments of the church cannot be looked upon as a " system " in the sense of some merely mechanistic, legalistic, narrowly understood set of forms, which can operate apart from, or in distinction from, the life of the whole body. So to regard them would be to change them into magic and forget that their significance, and their only significance, is to serve Christ's living purpose of incorporating men into himself.

Here as so often I find myself drawn greatly toward the Eastern Orthodox view. But it is also noteworthy that the liturgical movement in all parts of the Western church and the writings of many other theologians who are not themselves necessarily influenced by its ideals but are concerned with the implications of the Pauline teaching about the body of Christ show a similar tendency to stress this organic notion of sacraments and to use for its description language which is neither mechanistic nor purely " spiritual," but quite plainly and frankly vitalistic. I admit that there is a danger in this biological emphasis, so common in our time; but I believe that it is the most fruitful and useful of all the ways of approaching a right and nourishing understanding of the church and the sacraments, provided we never minimize the place of reason, on the one hand, nor seek a merely pragmatic sanction for our religious life, on the other.

We are now prepared to turn to the specific Christian sacraments. A sacrament in the particular Christian sense is a corporeal or material element or action which presents to the senses, shows by similarity, signifies by institution, and conveys by consecration, a spiritual grace intended by God for man. There are several important matters to be borne in mind here. The first is that the conventional Western definition of the number of sacraments as two or as seven was reached at a comparatively late date. Institution by our Lord himself has been the usual criterion; but as a result of modern Biblical criticism it can hardly be affirmed with certainty that he instituted in any *formal* sense any of the sacraments or sacramental rites, although (to employ the valuable Roman Catholic distinction) it may be said that all were instituted *in genere,* that is, by the general intention, in the divine purpose of the Eternal Word, incarnate in Jesus Christ, of establishing a society in which man's salvation would be accomplished with the employment of such means as properly and directly developed from actions or words of Jesus during the days of his flesh. A second point is that the efficacy of the sacraments, that is, the objective power or operation of God through the sacrament, depends on the divine will and not on the human agent who celebrates them. God will act efficaciously in answer to human prayer, but the answer is given by God, and hence *assuredly* given when that is done which ought to be done to indicate the petition to which the grace is the answer. Hence the sacraments depend so on God's will (but on no human control of God's will, which is absurd) that in at least one sense they are effective *ex opere operato*. This is a much misunderstood doctrine, but all it really means is that as in our general experience in the realm of the naturally sacramental the reality is *there* and possesses its reality because God is active and not because we *feel* its reality, so in the specific Christian sacrament God is first and God is trustworthy. On the other hand, the element of appropriation, response, assimilation, is our own invaluable contribution; it is required for the " beneficial effect " it exerts on human receptivity, or, in ordinary language, it is necessary for " worthy " reception. This is not magic, for in no sense at all is it suggested that man has control over the divine power, will, or presence. It simply brings the Christian sacraments into line with our general experience in which, unless we are entirely projectionist in theory, we recognize that human response is made to what is actually *there* to be received, to what is really done or truly present in the vast range of our human and physical environment.

A third point concerns the usual " parts " of a sacramental action. Sacraments obviously demand an outward sign, which involves some material thing or visible action whose purpose is to indicate the intention of God in Christ to act graciously. Related to this, words must be said which state that intention. Furthermore, sacraments include also the inward part or grace which is indeed " objectively present " but which must be " subjectively " received. And sacraments also require a competent minister to celebrate them — which means that they should be performed by one who as the representative or functioning agent of the body of Christ has been appointed to carry out this specific task. All this, I suggest, is part of that normal, orderly, healthy functioning which is essential to the integrity of the church in serving Christ's purpose.

It remains to make some brief comments on sacramental worship and life as a whole.

First, I should wish to emphasize again the aptness of the

Christian sacraments to the life of man. Living in a sacramental world, himself a sacramental being, he is met in the Christian church with a way of religious expression and evocation that is natural to him. In this connection I delight in the words spoken by my revered master in theology, Dr. Marshall Bowyer Stewart: " It is ever most natural for the Supernatural to be known and to work naturally." The church's sacraments are no adventitious or arbitrary intrusion into the world; they are what a priori we might have expected if Christianity is true at all and if it is based upon an action of God such as Christians assert occurred in the incarnation.

Secondly, it is important to stress the social nature of the sacraments of the Christian church. As the church is the body of Christ, so its sacraments are sacraments *of the body*. They are effective only because they are thus of the body; they are rightly received and used only by those who belong to the body, either in intention or in fact. When Paul speaks of the dreadful consequences to be expected by those who receive the Lord's Supper without discerning the Lord's body, I fancy that he was really saying that those who receive them without true " social " participation, without brotherhood, without faithful membership in the mystical body as at least intentional in their participation, eat and drink " damnation," which, in William Morris' telling phrase, is *nothing but* the " absence of fellowship." Such an insistence upon sociality is imperative, above all, in such sacraments or sacramentals as baptism, confirmation, holy orders, and absolution. It is easy enough to see its necessity in the other three — marriage, anointing, and the Holy Eucharist; but it must be emphasized particularly in the first group of sacramental actions, whose point is that they relate men, in one way or another, for one purpose or another, in response to one need or another, to the life of the total body of Christ.

The ancient sacramental life and actions of the church have another quality to which we alluded briefly at the end of the last chapter. They parallel, with amazing precision, the great moments and the great needs in the lives of men. As men are born, so are they baptized into the family of Christ; as they grow up to need strengthening for full responsible action, so they are confirmed; as they fall into error and stray from the right, so they are shriven; as they require nourishment day by day to live nobly, and some cause to which they can give their lives, so they receive Holy Communion and are incorporated in Christ's self-offering; as they establish their own little communities of love and family care, so they marry with the blessing of God through the church; as they are ill in body and presently must die, so they are anointed when ill and prepared for the death which is the lot of every man. Similarly, as they seek the more nearly to serve God, so they are called to the general Christian vocation and in certain instances to a specific vocation in the body of Christ as its ministers. For a discussion of this entire question, I would refer to a noble book by Dietrich von Hildebrand, *Liturgy and Personality*.[15]

We have said little in detail about the particular sacraments, by which we become " very members incorporate in the mystical body of Christ," and by which we are strengthened and nourished. It is the peculiar privilege of the Christian to live consciously as a sacramental being in a world that is sacramental and through his worship to realize more deeply his own sacramental nature. If there were no other proof to be offered of the general truth of the Christian position here, this would seem to me to be almost enough to convince one of it. Miss Underhill, in her striking book, *Man and the Supernatural,* wrote: "Through the Christian sacraments that self-giving, of which the incarnation is the supreme example, finds another and continuous expression: sense here becoming the vehicle through which the very Spirit of life enters into the little lives of men." [16] So intimately, so precisely, so entirely does this dovetail with our own general human experience, that it would be incredible for it not to be credible.

5

The Meaning of Man's Sexuality

We turn now to still another aspect of man's existence which is closely related to his embodiedness and his social belonging. In the schema proposed in our introductory chapter, this is the sixth statement in the description of human nature: that man is a sexual being.

But before we begin our discussion, there is an important point that must be made, because any consideration of human sexuality would be put in the wrong context without it; and the point is that the several statements about man which so far have been made are essentially *cumulative in nature.* That is to say, we must begin by seeing man as a creature, a dependent being; we must then go on to recognize that in his dependency he is possessed of a drive for fulfillment in God, a dynamic quality of a kind that marks him off from other instances of creaturehood. After this, we must see that he is so much a social being, finding his meaning only when he is aware of his relationship with others of his race, that he can never be understood, or understand himself, in simply individualistic terms. Finally, we must recognize his embodied nature, the fact that he is not a mind or soul that happens to be resident temporarily in a physical body, but rather that he is himself a mind-body unity. In Gabriel Marcel's phrase,

he does not " have " a body, he " is " a body — although
that is not all there is to be said about him, since he is both
possessed of a spiritual nature and related to God in a very
special way — not only is he able to establish some sort of
relationship with divine Reality but he is so made that his
only adequate fulfillment is *in* God as his final " end."

We rightly approach the sexuality which is integral to
human nature when, and only when, these prior facts are
kept in mind. For despite much contemporary thinking
and writing human sexuality is not identical with the
sexuality common to other biological species. I once said
at a conference of university students that " man is very
definitely a sexual being and can be understood only when
this is taken into account." One of the students spoke up
promptly, saying, " So are apples." Of course apples are
sexual; but man is sexual in a different sense from an apple
— and from an ape too. He is a human being, not an apple
or an ape; his sexuality is distinctively human. In him the
sexual nature that is found in almost all living matter is
characterized by the special human qualities and the peculiarly human overtones of meaning of which we have
been speaking in the earlier chapters of this book.

We shall return to this in the sequel. But for the moment
it is important to emphasize that human sexuality is indeed much more than the biological drive for the propagation of the species. It is easy to see that it is not simply another instance of the animal procreative instinct, for it is
other than the occasional " rutting " common to animals.
Human sexuality is intimately part of the human dyna-
mism for self-fulfillment; and this is apparent in the experience of men and women, who at their best are not content unless in some fashion they can experience " love " and
" self-giving " in their sexual relationships. Their biologi-

cal instinct of propagation is incorporated in a different context from "rutting" habits; that context includes a yearning for self-realization, a desire for full actualization of what it means to be human, and this incorporation of the biological instinct in a wider context gives it a new significance, a new direction, and a new dimension. Even when human sexuality seems simply to be lust, nothing but the "rutting" of which we have spoken, and without love in any significant sense, we can time and again see how it shows itself to be more than that merely animal function. The proof of this is found in the dis-ease, the dissatisfaction, sometimes even the keen sense of guilt, which attaches to human sexuality when it is indulged without controls of any kind and with no sort of "self-giving." Despite the strenuous efforts of some psychologists, it seems impossible for this guilt to be explained away, any more than we can explain away dis-ease and dissatisfaction, by reason of supposed pressure or accepted social patterns. Modern psychological study would appear to demonstrate, beyond any shadow of doubt, that man simply cannot be just an animal, try as hard as he will; and sexual malaise is not like a slight illness that a competent physician can heal. It is much more like a ravaging and fatal disease.

In considering the Christian interpretation of human sexuality, it will be helpful to begin with a few preliminary remarks whose importance will soon appear.

Every Christian conviction takes its origin from the revealing action of God, known to man in human history or in the world of nature. That is why the Christian understanding of human nature, and hence of human sexuality, must constantly be referred back both to God's general action in the world and also to the incarnation and the atonement, in which events Christians believe God took supreme action for man. We have already emphasized the extraordinary fact that the view of man which follows from the Christian faith is in remarkable correspondence with that picture of man which careful observation and scientific inquiry force upon us. So there are really two bases for the Christian understanding of man's sexuality: one is the revelation of God in Christ, the other is the result of our attempt reasonably to understand ourselves and our brethren in the light of such knowledge as we possess apart from that " special " revelation.

This is not the place, nor need we spend the time, for a detailed consideration of the relation of man's reason and God's revelation. It must suffice to say that there is no necessary contradiction between these two, although the Christian faith is indeed based primarily on revelational events rather than on human reason. Neither need we say more about the problem of " special " and " general " revelation than that the term " general revelation " may rightly be taken to denote such knowledge of God as we may receive through the study of the impact upon men of the natural order and the average " run " of human history, while " special revelation " may properly be seen in those particular and focal events, or series of events, which by their intensity and fruitfulness have become " important " for men, and may therefore be used as tests and criteria for the remainder of our experience. For our purpose in this chapter, it is sufficient that we recognize the interplay of revelation and reason, and of general and special revelation, without being obliged to resort at every point to a careful discrimination between what is inevitably " of faith " and what is " from reason " or knowledge derived from God's more widely diffused revelatory action.

From our Christian theological background we may draw

some conditions that will prepare the way for our picture of man as sexual. Some of these we have already treated at length, but it will be useful to set them all down in a series:

1. In the revelation of God in Christ, human nature has been used by the divine Reality in a sacramental fashion. That is to say, an " outward and visible " thing, a genuine and complete human life, was taken for the instrumental expression of an " inward and spiritual " Reality, God himself. Human nature was not destroyed or damaged by this operation; rather, it was perfected and brought to its fullest flower.

2. The whole process of creation, as well as the action of redemption, is sacramental in nature. Divine purposes, spiritual values and meaning, are at work in and through tangible, sensible realities. Our only way of knowing the former is through the latter: we have never seen love, but only loving actions. Whatever meaning there may be in the universe is known to us in, through, and under the material embodiments of that meaning which we see, feel, hear.

3. The Christian church conceived as the body of Christ is a dual reality, in which spiritual life works through, because it is present in, a visible human institution. The body of Christ is expressed in a body of men. The church as *corpus Christi* is corporately operative: and the two sides are related in so direct and intimate a fashion that one cannot be had without the other.

4. Christian worship is at its height in the Eucharist or Holy Communion, where bread and wine, physical things, are the instrumental media for the spiritual reality of the " body and blood " — that is, the true life — of the risen Christ for those who are members of his church.

To these Christian theological statements we must add the further assertions from the realm of ordinary human experience and scientific investigation, to which we have drawn attention in earlier chapters of this book:

1. Man is an elaborately contrived organism in which mind and body appear to be so much a unity one with the other that human psychology and human physiology are not susceptible, in any final sense, of isolated treatment.

2. Whatever may be said of occasional reported instances of " extrasensory perception," it is by and large true that human experience is initially sensory. It may not be absolutely the case, but it is certainly largely the case, that nothing is in the mind which is not first in the senses. Our minds get to work on and react upon presentations of physical experience developed through the several senses, however many and various these senses may be.

3. The advance made in the treatment of the ills of human personality since the advent of a psychosomatic picture of man are so enormous that we cannot be sure whether mind or body is the basic seat of many human ailments. It has long been known that anxiety and peptic ulcers were closely related; now we know that many other bodily disorders have their root in mental disturbances, and vice versa.

4. Man's embodiedness includes not only his own physical body but also the body corporate. The human race is so ordered that men form a social whole, living with, and indeed living in, their fellowmen. It is not good for man to be alone; and God has set the solitary in families. This is both a natural and spiritual truth.

5. Common sense has never doubted that physical expression of mental and spiritual states is both necessary and desirable. The young man who tells his beloved that he loves her is acting naturally and (within whatever limits we may believe proper) desirably when he expresses this

fact by kissing her. Patriotism is naturally and rightly shown by acts of reverence to the queen or by a salute to the flag. When children, challenged about the truth of a statement they have made, make a gesture that is described by them with the words, " Cross my heart and hope to die," they are acting perfectly normally, properly, and naturally.

Now all of these facts about man are the background for the view of human nature which is integral to the total Christian conception of the meaning of existence, and that view of human nature is the necessary presupposition for the Christian understanding of human sexuality. It has been a serious defect in much of the writing and thinking on this subject even among Christians that it has failed to begin with this wide theological background, and has started instead either with the observation of men's sexual behavior (as in the Kinsey Report [17]) or with a set of supposed arbitrary divine commands or moral imperatives which it is thought should govern such behavior. In consequence, the whole enterprise has been unrelated to the basic facts of the nature of man and the meaning of his existence under God. No wonder, then, that the discussion has tended either toward " idealism," on the one hand, or to " practical realism," on the other. The former is so much in the clouds that it appears to have very little connection with the concrete experience of men and women; while the latter is so much concerned with " right sexual adjustments " that it seems to be without any criteria of judgment and hence to be pragmatic in the most obvious and indeed superficial sense.

For the Christian the starting point for a discussion of sexuality must be theological in the broadest sense; and the theology is reasonably developed in the context of general human experience and its meaning. This is why the Christian begins by saying that man is a body-mind organism, living in a community with other men. He is himself a sacramental creature, in whom spiritual states, thoughts, feelings, aspirations, are expressed through a physical instrument; on the other hand, the things done with and by the body are profoundly related to, and have enormous consequences for, that which goes on in the mind or soul of " personality." And this construction of human nature is no accident, but is integrally related to the nature of the universe itself and to the way in which God works in it to accomplish his purposes.

Man's corporeal life, as the instrumental means for his spiritual and mental life, is intimately bound up (as we have seen) with the fact of his corporate existence. The individual human being is hardly a man, in the true sense of the word, unless he is in real community with his fellows. The word " person " is not to be taken as if it were but a synonym for " individual." The latter describes *one instance* of a given species: a man, a dog, a stone, an electron. But the word " person " describes an instance of a given species — namely, man — who possesses the capacity to enter into relationship with another of his kind; and the relationship is such that a warm, self-giving, shared experience is possible, without loss of the self and yet with communion of that self with others. In a word, person means " individual in community." Man's sacramental nature, therefore, as we have stressed again and again, is both corporeal and corporate, through a *physical* body and in a *social* body.

There are two dangers that dog the endeavor to understand the sexual side of our human existence. Each comes from an attempt to build too exclusively on one aspect of our nature. If we devote our time and attention solely to the physical body, we are likely to reduce the functioning of human personality to sheer animalism, in which man is thought of, and even treated, as if he were only another beast. The consequences of this procedure, in the area of sexual expression, are obvious and terrible. But if we give our whole thought to the mental or spiritual side of man, we are quite as likely to fall into frightful error. For we shall then be victims of what we have already styled " angelism," thinking of man as if he were pure spirit without body. And the consequences of this procedure in the realm of sexuality are again obvious and terrible. A futile and self-destroying negation of the body brings about a warping and perverting of the spirit, with an ugliness that in some instances (as shown, say, in François Mauriac's *Woman of the Pharisees* [18]) is even worse than the results of animalism.

A similar danger is manifested in still another way as between man as an individual and man in community. If the uniting concept of person, meaning individual in community, is forgotten, we may attend exclusively to one or the other of the two terms. We may concern ourselves exclusively with the individual, forgetting the social medium which is essential to man's self-expression. In consequence, the horrors of " rugged individualism " will appear, with selfish, grasping efforts after " one's own good " and a callous disregard for the " good of others." But on the other hand, an exclusive interest in community can be equally dangerous, for this reduces man to an ant in an anthill, a bee in the hive, whose only purpose and function is to be part of a social order which can be served without concern for the single man or for his freedom and his happiness. That way lies fascism and the totalitarian state, in whatever guise (even a " democratic " one) it may present itself. The bearing of these dangers upon sexual life is clear enough. When man's sexual nature is expressed without regard for the society in which he lives and of which as person he is a part, we have that unregulated individualistic exploitation of others which makes for chaos and anarchy — man becomes a selfish philanderer. But it is also true — and this is perhaps the explanation of much of the demand for " sexual freedom " — that conformity to purely conventional social patterns can be destructive of the spontaneity of the person who feels that he is buried under the mores and can never know the joyous release of true sexual give-and-take. A man or woman cannot be himself in such a situation, but must always be submerged in the pressure toward simple conformity with what are assumed to be the larger interests of society.

What is required to do justice to all the facts is a view of man as person in community, compounded of soul and body, placed in a context in which he can be himself, as created by God, but freed from both the ulterior drives of sheer individuality and also the accumulated repressions of a closed society. In religious language, he needs to be released from the incubus of sin, both inherited and actual, placed in the state of grace or freedom under God, and empowered to live according to God's will. But this is an impossibility for him, so far as his own efforts go. He must *be released;* he must *be placed* in grace; he must *be empowered.*

This need for restoration is intimately connected with man's sexuality although it is not expressed through that alone. The fact that man is a sexual animal is not in itself an evil thing. On the contrary, it is a good thing, for sexuality, like everything else given by God in creation, is good in and of itself. Yet the first two possibilities — that man may either attempt to act as sheer animal *or* pretend that he can act as sheer spirit — and the second pair of possibilities — that he may live as a " rugged individual " with utter disregard for his brethren's good *or* may lose himself in his social environment so that he becomes no more than a cog in the social machine — present obvious occasions for sin on man's part. These occasions can be, and have been, used by man to deny his God-given nature in all its richness and complexity. And the point in human life where such negation can be expressed most obviously, although of course in no sense exclusively, is the sexual realm. This distortion can therefore be taken, as it was taken by Augustine fifteen hundred years ago and by Sigmund Freud in our own time, as a symbol of the wider fact of the distortion of personality which Christians call sin.

Such distortion is not " total depravity," as this has commonly been understood. It is, rather, a distortion of every area of man's experience, total only in the sense that it is found in each part of his existence rather than confined to some single aspect such as will or emotion. But there remains always basic to man that connection with God which comes from the truth of his creation " in the divine image " and his grounding in the Word of God who is " the Light, which lighteth every man."

When man is freed from his sin, he is enabled to " transcend himself " without denying or neglecting any area of his existence as this is given by God. Apart from such restoration by God, his capacity to rise above his immediate experience and view his life from a quasi-transcendent perspective is itself indeed the chief occasion for his willfulness. Nowhere is this more completely shown than in the arrogance of the Casanova or the hypocrisy of the Pharisee.

Man, then, needs restoration. Nothing in him needs destruction; but his sinful affections and desires, with their rooting in his willful mind and proud spirit, must be reoriented and centered in God so that they are no longer sinful. What is needed is the bringing back of human existence to the pattern set for it by Reality, by God. The ancient prayer in the Roman liturgy for the blessing of the water to be used in the Eucharistic chalice puts this admirably: " O God, who didst wonderfully create the dignity of man's nature and still more wonderfully hast restored it. . . ." This *dignitas* — this rightful ordering, in a place of honor in God's creation — is what human nature has lost by its sin; its restoration will bring about the healthy and natural functioning of man as son of God, according to God's intention and in agreement with God's will for his children.

For this reason, the attempts of many anthropologists, sociologists, biologists, etc., to discuss man's sexuality in terms merely of its " fallen " (that is, observable) expression is entirely beside the point. So also is the confusion of " normal " in the sense of " what everybody does " with " normal " in the sense of that which man as true man should do and be. To reduce morality to " observed " behavior is to destroy morality itself. What is even more significant, it is to destroy the peculiarly *human* element in human nature, since the distinctive thing about man is his double awareness, both of his possible perfection and of his appalling distance from that possibility. It is difficult to have patience with the many writers on sexual matters who seem unable to recognize that there is a difference between " typical animal " and " normal human " expressions of sexuality. Nor need we wonder that as a result of their failure to see this difference, they often talk as if the solution of the problem of man's sexuality were the behavior of the stud farm, with a little gleam of spurious idealism to relieve the sheer animality of such brute behavior.

There is a final point that is central to the whole Christian outlook. Man is made for God. We have quoted Augustine's " Thou hast made us for thyself, O Lord, and our heart is restless until it rest in thee." Yet as we have pointed out, the translation that we have just given, found in nearly all English versions, does not do justice to the rich sense of the original. Augustine should be translated as saying: " Thou hast made us to move toward, grow toward, live toward, develop toward thee. . . ." His conception is not static; it is deeply dynamic. God has planted in us a strong and irresistible drive toward himself. If this drive were permitted to have its way with us, we should find the " rest " in God which is the goal of our human striving and the full satisfaction and completion of every area and aspect of our human personality. Since we do not permit this free work of God in us, we are disordered, unintegrated, warped, and perverted.

Man's sexuality is so deep and real a part of human nature that of all expressions of man's existence it can best be taken as a central symbol of his personality. It is natural, then, that it should have its enormous place in that movement toward God or that movement toward self, which Augustine describes as the twin possibilities for man. So sexuality visibly manifests, in many instances, the total orientation of the personality. The great bishop's well-known definitions, found in his *The City of God,* of the two loves by which we live will help us here. He spoke, it will be recalled, of " love of God to the contempt of self," and " love of self to the contempt of God." [19] But the " self " which is to be held in contempt by a true man is not the *genuine* self, the God-intended person in its rich fulfillment in community. It is, on the contrary, the *immediate* self which desires, without ordering or control, to secure its own way and achieve its own ends, thereby losing all that is really good and gaining only the hell of self-disintegration. But when God is loved, to the contempt of *that* self, the genuine self is realized, for the drive of the personality is at one and the same time toward the fulfillment of the genuine self which is the ultimate meaning of human existence on the terrestrial level.

Thus in the sexual life, sexual " satisfaction " when sought for its own sake, without regard for the pattern in which it is placed and the purpose for which it exists, is destructive. In the long run it can produce only dust and ashes, and in the end disintegration of human personality and human society. But when sought in the right pattern, ordered according to the God-given structure of human life, it can and does play its significant and sacramental role in the movement of man's personality toward his chief good. It enriches his experience and brings him deep and lasting joy. For it is eternally true, despite much current theological writing, that *erōs* and *agapē* — the first, the love of desire; the second, self-giving love — are not utterly separate and mutually contradictory. *Erōs* may be purified and refined in the fire of the divine *Agapē*. In the idiom of the great African saint whom we have quoted so often, the divine *caritas* (love can redeem human *amor* (desire) , so that the resulting human *dilectio* (delight) in loving will be the holy desire which finds rest and satisfaction in the heavenly *Caritas,* in God himself.

Perhaps the point of our discussion up to now will be made more clearly if we attempt to put it in yet another way.

We have been saying over and over again that man is a body-mind unity, a psychosomatic being; we have also said that he is made for fulfillment in community, that is, he needs others in order truly to *be* himself. And we have repeated again and again that these two facts about man are peculiarly relevant when we come to think of sexuality in that special quality which attaches to it as found in humankind. Because man is a psychosomatic being, he expresses himself through the employment of physical media. What precisely these media may be, in this or that particular instance, is not now to the point; the simple truth is that his body is for him the instrument for his self-expression. But we need also to remember that man is so made that for his achievement of proper humanity he requires fulfillment, and this cannot be true of him only in a spiritual sense; it must be equally true of him in a physical sense, for there is no contradiction between these two nor is there any separation of them. In every action of man, as we now know him, both sides of the unity are engaged. Man is so made that in chemical, biological, psychological, and spiritual ways he is at unity in himself; his chemistry, biology, and psychology, as well as his spirituality, are not segmented fragments. They all go to make up his total personality, the unity that is his as man.

Thus at the level of the strictly physical and biological, man possesses both the biological drives and the physical organs which are directed toward his proper fulfillment — fulfillment, in this case, in another of his own race. The Bible itself tells us that God created man " male and female," that is, he created man with precisely such a drive for physical fulfillment. Psychologically, too, man has the drive for fulfillment with another on the emotional level; this has been brought home to us lately with singular clarity, through the recent studies that have been made of the depths of personality and of those levels of personality which are above as well as those which are below the frontier of consciousness. Furthermore, man is made for fulfillment in God — here there is a religious drive for what we might describe as " spiritual " fulfillment, or perhaps we might more accurately say fulfillment on the spiritual level of his total personal life. Now all of these drives fit together in a single pattern; all are included when we speak of the dynamics of human personality. Man as a psychosomatic unity, in community with his fellows, is then the creature who seeks in that very unity to secure such fulfillment as shall satisfy him on every level. The whole of man's embodiedness is included in his urge to fulfill himself.

But we have also seen that man is man only insofar as he realizes the truth of his social belonging, his life in community. Nobody can live without his fellows. It is therefore highly significant that human sexuality is the way of the deepening of the social relationship that is part of human nature; it is even more important that it is the way of carrying that relationship above the level of simple belonging to the level of the sharing which we call love — the giving of self to another self that also gives. Here human sexuality is intimately and inextricably part of the social nature of man; for in the sexual drive for fulfillment in another of his race, man's established sociological reality is made deeper, richer, more profoundly expressive of himself.

Thus we have another proof of the fact that human sexuality is representative of the double truth about humanity: first, that it is embodied and that it is social; and second, that it is expressive of the basic drive in him to find a fulfillment that will enrich and complete his life. Here is confirmation of the Christian position about man's sexuality. It is a good thing in itself, although certainly it can be misused, misdirected, distorted, and twisted. It is a natural part of man and its satisfaction is proper to man. But the Christian view goes much deeper even than that, since it affirms that human sexuality reveals its highest significance, its most profound purpose, when it is related to God himself. *This* is the meaning in human sexuality which lifts it entirely above, even while it remains grounded in, the sexual instinct that men share with apples and apes. For the ultimate goal of all man's sexual activity, when rightly and proportionately understood, is nothing other than God himself. This is a way of saying that it is only through fulfillment in God, in company with one's fellows, that one can receive in the fullest sense that satisfaction which sexuality in its own sphere and on its own level provides through a fellow human being who acts as a surrogate — although never as a substitute, save when sexuality is misdirected and misused — for God himself. This is why for the Christian the sexual relationship must be sacramentally defined. It is " an outward and visible sign," to use again the language of the catechism in *The Book of Common Prayer,* " of an inward and spiritual " reality: a sign, symbolic and effectual, not only of the love that two human beings have one for the other, but also a sign, symbolic and effectual, of the love that is God-given and that ultimately is nothing else than God himself.

This helps us to see why the Christian church condemns promiscuity, or what moral theologians would call sexual inordination — sexuality without proper ordering and direction. This inordination is not only morally wrong, in that it defies the mores of a given society or culture; but it

is also, and for the Christian church much more significantly, destructive of personality in its truest signification.
For the essence of love is that in its giving and receiving
there is complete mutuality and complete faithfulness: the
two parties to it are bound in one, through the act of sexual union, but this is possible only because of the identifica-
tion of the one with the other in that mutual " help " and
that self-surrender which are made real at the level of conscious and willed human " promise." Fidelity or faithfulness is at the heart of the truly human sexual relationship.
When that is found the other to whom one is bound becomes the sacramental representation and the given occasion for fulfillment with *the* Other who is God. This is
why monogamy is no mere accident of man's social history; it is the direction in which man through the course
of his historical development, under the guidance of God,
has come to the realization of the fullest possible self-giving
and self-fulfillment in lifelong faithful union of one with
another. The " end " of this relationship is that the " love
which moves the sun and the other stars " may be manifested and known in, through, and under the circumstances
of ordinary historical human living.

Failure to see what Christianity is driving at in its sexual teaching is responsible for a serious situation among
Christian people themselves, who often cannot recognize
why the church has taken such a high, and at the same time
such a disciplined, view of the matter. It is also responsible
for the failure on the part of many who are at least touched
by Christian ideas to see how enormously helpful to them
such an understanding of sexuality can be. For essentially
this Christian view has a healthy and wholesome attitude
to what sometimes is dismissed as a dirty or indecent part
of human life. So highly does Christianity value man's sex-

uality that it cannot permit it to be degraded to the level of animality or let it be denied in the supposed interest of a superior "spirituality." Sexuality in man, as everywhere else, is good; it is a means for self-fulfillment; ultimately it is a sign in man of the love of God and of God as love. But it can be abused and distorted, turned into animality, just as it can be denied and rejected and made into something that "nice" people do not like. Precisely because these two possibilities are ever with us, in our freedom as men, human sexuality must be ordered and directed aright lest what was meant to be human love, with its physical expression in sexual union, becomes bestial lust — in which the physical expression is given a place that is so dominant in and of itself that the fullness of personal relationship, under God, is denied and lost. It is this which Christian faith recognizes to be at stake.

That is why it is appropriate to say something further at this point about man in defection from his true self — and this before we come to the formal consideration of the theme in its proper place in our scheme. We have noted already that human sexuality can provide the easiest and most readily available means for that defection. Freud was right — perhaps more right than he could know — when he insisted that human sexuality, so deep in each of us, can be a way in which we damage our proper self-expression and thus impede our proper self-fulfillment. Of course, Freud did not develop any Christian consequences from this fact, which he had learned through his long clinical experience; but there is no reason why others, not victimized by Freud's nineteenth-century materialistic naturalism, may not do so. Indeed we have observed that Augustine did just this, centuries ago. Underneath Augustine's exaggerated distrust of sexuality, which was the product of his own bitter experience in early years, there is a profound truth. It is a tragedy that the great African theologian's insight and way of getting at the truth was so tied in with this distrust born of his experience that a terrible legacy of antisexualism has been handed down in some parts, but never in the normative and mainstream, of Christian thought. But with all his exaggerations he was trying to show that the area of human life in which man's proud self-assertion, his arrogance in claiming to " run the whole show," his refusal to accept and abide by his dependent status as a creature under God, is as a matter of observable fact readily, quickly, and appallingly given expression in the area of sexual relations. There can be no doubt at all — and the experience of man demonstrates this clearly — that we can and do claim, and act on the claim to, human self-sufficiency and human lordship over others; in sexual relationships we can seek to be lords of another human life, possessing that life (or trying to do so) without recognizing or admitting that all life is God's alone; declaring in action the independence and sovereignty, arrogated to oneself instead of given to God, which is the root and cause of all that is wrong about man.

Why is this so? I think that a popular song of many years ago will tell us. It spoke favorably of " *my* wanting what *I* want when *I* want it." But this way in which we try to run the world, and other people in the world, according to our own particular, limited, partial, inadequate, and defective notions is no good thing. It is a terrible perversion of human nature. And our sexuality when it is disordered and simply self-assertive is a great and dreadfully obvious sign of that perversion. One recognizes this when one reads some modern novels, where the whole purpose of existence seems sometimes to be the achievement of sexual experience without regard for consequences for personality, without regard for the full personal relationship that is implicit in all sexuality in man, without regard for the ultimate fulfillment of human life in God — however we may picture God and whatever may be the incognitos through which that fulfillment may be given.

I know of no more frightful picture of the destructive nature of human sexuality, when it is not ordered and channeled and when it is not seen in its proper context, than Jean-Paul Sartre's discussion of the sexual relationship in his celebrated *L'Etre et le néant*.[20] Despite all that is true and valuable in his pages, and there is much that is so, sexuality is portrayed as essentially the desire to possess and control another human being. The final result, as he shows it, is indeed "nothingness." In sexuality so conceived, Sartre gives us an entirely apt preview of his final conclusion about human life altogether; he states it on almost the last page of his book: "Man is a useless passion." [21] In striking contrast to Sartre, D. H. Lawrence saw deeply into what we have called the sacramental significance of human sexuality. In many of his stories and novels, frequently in his letters, but chiefly in *Lady Chatterley's Lover*,[22] human sexuality is portrayed as a vital participation in the dynamic force in the universe for giving and receiving, for love, for fulfillment. There is nothing of "useless passion" here; there is entrance into the deepest meaning of human existence — as Father Martin Jarrett-Kerr, C.R., has so well shown in his study of Lawrence's thought under the title *D. H. Lawrence and Human Existence*.[23] Nor is it without significance that it was a Christian monk who saw this in Lawrence. Doubtless Lawrence, in violent reaction against what he called the "white Christ" and in his revulsion from the puritanical negativism of his childhood experience in the midlands of England, was far too extreme in some of his assertions about sex. He represents a valuable protest, however, against the sexual anemia that some who have called themselves Christians have mistakenly thought to have the sanction and approval of Christian faith. And if his protest is extreme, it is at least corrective of that opposite fallacy, while on the other hand, it is a noble if very explosive assertion that sexuality is neither a mere animal function nor simply the way in which man, in his awful loneliness, tries to use another life without regard for mutuality and fidelity.

For the Christian, who knows what he is talking about when he speaks of human sexuality, there is here a sign and symbol, yes, a sacrament, of the love that is divine and that is God himself. Understood in that dimension, controlled and governed by the desire for genuine fulfillment in God — even if God is not named as such, but known only as the " third " who binds the two in one — sexuality is indeed a wonderful and a glorious thing. Human love, not in spite of but because of, not apart from but in, its physical expression in sexual union is a token and presence in our midst of the divine Charity. And love, so known, has about it the very quality of eternity.

6

Man in Defection from His True Self

In Albert Camus's novel *The Plague* there is a moving incident in which a doctor and a priest are in conversation. They have just left the bedside of a dying child, one of the many stricken by the plague in the Algerian city where they work. Both of them are " on edge " after their visit to the child. After some disagreement between them, the doctor breaks out: " I don't want to start a dispute with you. We are working together for something that unites us beneath our blasphemies and prayers. That's all that matters." To this the priest replies: " Yes, you also work for the salvation of man." The doctor tries to smile; he answers: " The salvation of man . . . that's too big a word for me. It's his health I'm interested in. His health, first of all." [24]

But the two men are really saying much the same thing, in at least one sense. They both recognize that man is sick. For one of them, the emphasis is on his sickness in body, for the other it is on his sickness in " soul " — or, as I should prefer to put it, his sickness in his total personality in all its relationships. Both see that what man needs is health, restoration to wholeness. As the doctor knows, man needs health of body, certainly; but as the priest knows, he also needs health in total personality — the wholeness which, whatever may be the etymological relation of the words, is " holiness."

The word " salvation," which the priest used, is derived from roots that mean health, sanity, welfare, integration. I quite realize the importance of Prof. James Barr's argument in his *The Semantics of Biblical Language* [25] that such etymological connections can be pushed to absurd lengths in theological discussion; yet I am sure that there is a truth in this particular derivation to which we must give most serious attention. And in any event, whatever may be the relationship of the meaning of the words as a matter of linguistic origin, the fact that today we are seeing more and more helpful cooperation between medical doctors, experts in psychology, students of cultural history and sociology, and theologians indicates that there is indeed a profound interrelationship of all these areas in their common concern for what we might appropriately style " the righting of human nature."

In his *Preces Privatae,* Bishop Launcelot Andrewes (that Caroline divine whose literary virtues have been so highly praised by T. S. Eliot) addresses God in these words: " Two things I recognize in myself, O Lord: the nature which thou hast made; the sin which I have added." [26] Here man is portrayed as good, because God has created him; yet he is portrayed as fallen into sin — sin that he himself has " added," something that is not true to man in the divine intention but that is true in his present existence and that therefore must be recognized and reckoned with. There is here also in the setting of Andrewes' words in prayer, an implicit corollary to which we shall turn our attention in the next chapter: that " the nature which God has made," and which man by his " addition " has spoiled, can be restored to man, enriched by its being crowned and fulfilled and brought to true excellence through what has been accomplished for man in Jesus Christ.

We hear a great deal in the Christian pulpit and in theological discussion these days about sin; sometimes one may think that we hear almost too much, for, after all, the Christian gospel is not so much about man's sin as it is about God's grace. It is not centered in the old Adam in whom we die, but in the new Adam in whom we are made alive. However this may be, we are in a period in which easy optimism has disappeared. We have nowadays only contempt for the age when it seemed possible to look upon man as needing only a little more education, a little more guidance here and there, for him to become a paragon of virtue. It is commonly agreed today that human life is twisted and distorted, affected by the accumulated heritage of human wrong-doing, perverted from its true end and goal so that it is well-nigh impossible for any of us to accomplish with any degree of success the right which is also our duty. And something like this, although certainly not the extreme pessimism so prevalent among us, is the truth.

It is not simply a matter of this and that particular bit of wrong-doing, wrong-thinking, wrong-speaking. It is a situation in which we find ourselves, much more profoundly than it is a series of acts which we commit. Prof. Roland Mushat Frye, in his book *Perspective on Man*,[27] has written: " Man's problem is not to be summarized in terms of a list of sins, not even in terms of that remarkably inclusive list of the seven deadly sins, for these sins are themselves the products of a deeply planted originating sin — a phrase which is, I think, more descriptive than original sin — and this originating sin is the creature's will to exist as his own god. The fall of man, by which man has perennially fallen and still falls, is the attempt to establish himself as his own god, and to claim for his own private dominion the fruit of the knowledge of good and evil. Man's assertion of his own deity is not made in terms of the naïve worship of an idol made in his own image, but expresses itself rather in his continual drive to establish himself as the determinative norm of whatever world he inhabits, and to extend the bounds of his habitation so as to extend the determinative power of his own will, bringing persons and things and truth and even God into subjection to himself. It is thus that man repudiates life in the image of God in order to live as god.

" That is what is expressed by the Genesis story of the fall of man. Adam, or *ādhām* in the Hebrew, is not a proper name restricted to one man . . . but a generic noun meaning man, or mankind, and the entire account refers to the total human condition rather than to a chronologically isolated event."

Here we have a particularly lucid statement of the point that we ourselves have sought to make clear in earlier chapters: that it is pride, refusal to accept his place in the scheme of things, which is basic to man's problem; and here too we have the recognition that the story in Genesis describing " the fall " is, like the story of man's creation in the same book, a story told about every man — a myth in the proper sense of the word. It is about *us* in our contemporary state that we are being instructed, not about some remote historical figure. And Dr. Frye goes on to say that it is " man's assumption of his own deity " which is " the frail substructure which renders his entire existence unstable, the origin of his alienation from God, from his neighbor, and from himself "; while he adds what later we shall reaffirm, that it is this " triple alienation which is broken by faith in the action of Christ."

So we come to the seventh in our series of assertions about man: he is in defection from himself; he is a sinner.

If there is any place where our description of man both as a social being and as an " amphibian " is peculiarly relevant, it is here. The fact that we live one with and one in another helps us toward understanding the way in which man's defection has spread through the whole race, while the embodiedness which is man's nature — his organic unity as mind and body — tells us that both his spiritual existence *and* his material existence are involved in this defection. It is indeed true that what are often called the " sins of the flesh " are less important than those which are called the " sins of the spirit," for our bodies do not sin; it is *we* who sin by our bodies. But when we say that *we* sin, we recognize that it is the *total man* who sins. Our bodies are not the simple explanation of our defection; yet they are the instruments through which, as a result of our wrong-choosing and because of the feebleness of our wills, we usually express that defection. Nor can we rest content in assuming that our sin, or defection, is simply a matter of our individual life; it has profound consequences for our fellowmen who inevitably are affected by it.

During the late nineteenth and early twentieth centuries, a theory of sin was developed in which it was thought that the sinfulness of man could adequately be explained as the remnant of the animal in him — sin was " the ape and the tiger " in man, which had not yet been entirely eradicated in the upward progress toward " spirit." F. R. Tennant has often been accused of teaching this view in his *The Concept of Sin*,[28] but it is untrue to say this even if some critics drew this conclusion from the use that certain theologians made of what he did say. They assumed, although Dr. Tennant was careful not to, that man's bodily or physical nature represented a kind of " drag " which prevented his spiritual nature, or mind, or soul, from expressing itself properly and freely. On the other hand, there has always been in the Christian tradition a sort of antinomian fringe, which has maintained that sin dwells only in the mind or spirit, not in the body. Hence some have felt that the body is irrelevant to the problem. This idea can bring several practical conclusions. One of them, obviously, is that the body may go its own way, without prejudice to the soul. The result is sheer libertinism. Another is that there can be no such thing as " social sin," in the sense of sin attacking the body politic; religion's only task, as Hitler could pleasantly hold, is to save men's souls, while the state or some other agency " takes over " for the body and for the body's extension in its social relationships. Here once again, we see what happens when "animalism," on the one hand, or " angelism," on the other, is taken as the truth about human nature.

The solution of the problem of the nature of sin, so far as it can be solved, rests in a broader and more organic picture of man, in which he is seen as mind-body. When we take *this* as the truth, we are in no danger of sliding over into a dismissal of sin as merely a bodily " hangover," nor of treating man as if his " spiritual " nature were all that matters. And again, when we recognize that man is a total organism, in organic relationship to his society in which he finds the ground and expression for his life, we are delivered from the false abstraction that would treat him as if he could be " saved " in isolation from the community. Extricationist doctrines of salvation root back in fatal dichotomies set up in man's nature. Man as sinner is not a solitary sinner; he sins as a member of society, and the sins of his brethren in the corporate life of society are reflected in him and work upon him. To understand this is to come closer to grasping the real meaning of the miscalled doctrine of original sin. Man is indeed in a state of alienation from God's will for him, he is not acting as human nature is intended to act; but this is not true of him as an isolated monad. It is true of him in his deep social rootedness.

Hence the reform of the social order is necessarily included in the removal of man's sinfulness. It is absurd to talk as if man could be brought *out of* his social environment, just as it is absurd to attempt to remove him from his body. The pressures upon his physical nature, and his actions through that nature, are not irrelevant to the total human community which is in defection from the will of God; they are integral to that common humanity. Man sins in and with his mind, certainly, since his mind is the peculiarly " engineering " element in his personality; on the other hand, he sins by and through his body, since even in the most " spiritual " sins — as for instance, pride and selfishness — the organism is involved. And his body here includes the body corporate as well as the body corporeal. In any sinful deed, his body in this extended sense must to some degree be used for whatever expression there is; and his body in the same extended sense is affected by what he does. The body of man is inescapably *there,* both in his good creative actions and in his evil works.

We may therefore define sin as that which contradicts the true — that is, the divinely intended — nature of man, as mind-body in social relationships. Such a contradiction is the violation of the will of God. Sin is no arbitrary cate-

gory devised by God for reasons best known to himself and
not disclosed to men; rather, it is the denial of the actual
purpose of things according to the divine will — a purpose
that demands that *everything be itself,* what it is made to
be, to the limit of its capacity and in accord with its particular nature. *Particular* sins are the one-after-another
instances of man's *general* failure — in mind, in body, in
society — to be *himself.* Here, we may suggest, there is
opened a fruitful line of inquiry, in which the testimony
of the several sciences as well as the witness of Christian
theology can play a significant part. Such a book as Sir
Charles Sherrington's *Man on His Nature* [29] offers much
food for thought on this matter; so does an insistence, like
William James's, on the way in which the evil that men
do may be forgotten in their minds, and forgiven by their
God, but will still persist in the depths of their physical
nature. One of the few books that seems to take all this
into account is a small study by Prof. Robert L. Calhoun,
of Yale Divinity School, simply entitled *What Is Man?* [30]
The problem of man as sinner is but one of the fields in
which new insight may be gained and considerable advance accomplished by taking " man the amphibian "
very seriously indeed. It was one of the glories of the ancient Jewish faith that it held firmly to this conception;
the Christian church inherited it and maintained it, until
what Dr. Temple taught us to call " the Cartesian ' faux
pas ' " cut mind and body asunder, and individualistic
economic theories with their social concomitants divided
man from society. We are on the way back to an integral
view of man's body, man's soul, and man's society. When
we have succeeded in achieving this synthesis, we shall
have taken one of the most important steps toward a re-
establishment of the Christian world view.

Once again, it may be helpful for our understanding to approach the problem of sin from still another angle, in order to make quite clear the point that we are attempting to make. And this second line of approach may also deliver us from the temptation to fall back, for an excuse, on the patent fact of our sinful *situation* when we know ourselves to be guilty of this and that *particular* act of wrong-doing.

Christian theology, as we have seen, has talked much about something it calls " original sin." The phrase is not a happy one; indeed, it is an inaccurate one to describe the phenomenon it was intended to describe. But the fact that it does describe, however ineptly, is much worse than the word itself. We can call this fact, with Immanuel Kant, " radical evil "; we can call it, with Søren Kierkegaard, the great Danish thinker who has been rediscovered in our day, " inherited sinfulness "; with Paul Tillich and others we can speak of human estrangement from self, from others, and from God or from the " ground of our being." Whatever language we may wish to use, the terrible truth to which it points is the same. The human race, in some way or other, is caught in a situation in which its members simply are not able to " do the things they ought to have done " and to leave " undone the things they ought not to have done." The Anglican Prayer Book, which I have here quoted and paraphrased, goes on to say that " there is no health in us." That is an even more startling phrase than " original sin "; but what it is asserting is that in *us,* in man as he is at this present moment, there is a sickness, a disease, which prevents him from being whole or healthy; he lacks integration with the excellence that is his true end or purpose in being, and, above all, he lacks integration with the Excellence that is God himself.

I have already pointed out that the root evil in man is

his pride — his presumptuous attempt to claim that the whole universe revolves around his little self. He lives in terms of the pretension that he is an independent being, self-explanatory, able to get on quite satisfactorily just as he is and without any assistance from anywhere else. The consequence of this attempt to live on the basis of that radically false assumption is that he is, in Luther's words, " twisted in on himself " (*incurvatus in se*). To live like that means that he has deprived himself of the good that was intended for him; in the language of the medieval Scholastics, he is *privatus boni,* deprived of the true good that is proper to him — fulfillment in God and in God only. But also because of that, as the same Scholastics also said, he is *vulneratus in naturalibus,* wounded in the things natural to him as man. He cannot deprive himself of his true human good without at the same time seriously damaging the natural elements and areas in his life. Thus he is unable to think without prejudice; he is unable to love without false self-seeking; he is unable to will completely that which would bring him abiding joy. He cannot see things in the right way, as they actually are; he sees them as they affect *him*. He cannot act as he ought, because his warped desires get in his way. He cannot be the kind of being he was made to be.

Now some think that this is far too depressing a picture. It is indeed depressing, from one point of view; but the real question is not how depressing it may be, but how true it is. I believe it to be true. Yet I do not think that we ought, or need, to carry the picture to the point of looking at man as a *massa perditionis,* a rotten mass, in Augustine's phrase. Shakespeare has told us that " there is some soul of goodness in things evil "; but it is not we, it is God, who has the " patience to distil it out." And this means that even in our defection we are *not* totally lost, *entirely* without God, given up by our Maker and hence "without hope." There have been some Christian theologians who have talked like that, but they do not represent the main trend of Christian thought. That main trend has indeed recognized the facts, but it has never forgotten that even in his defection man is still the creature of God — if God were not there, man could not even exist. Neither has it forgotten that there is some working of God, some hidden operation of the divine Word, in the secret depths of every human life. As we saw in our earlier chapters, there is in man a potentiality which in Christ is made an actuality; this is sonship to God in fulfillment of our capacity for life in God. Sin can damage, and damage very seriously, that potentiality; but it can never destroy it, for if it did, man would be thoroughly irredeemable — and this the authentic Christian faith has *never* said.

Yet sin is not only a state or situation in which we find ourselves. It is also expressed in concrete actuality in the things we do, and say, and think; the things which it is not proper to us as men to do, and say, and think, because they deny our true nature as men and thus violate the will of God which is that we are to be men and nothing else. Nor are we able to claim, when we do these things or say these things or think these things, that we are not at all responsible; we cannot claim that "we were made that way." We were not *made* that way; that is not the truth about us but rather it is what we have done to make ourselves liars. To fall back on the childish plea, "I can't help it," is to deny our manhood.

Of course it is true that one of the unhappy by-products of recent psychological study and of the awareness it has given us of the factors that go to make us up has been a lessening of the sense of moral responsibility in many men and women. Doubtless it will take some little time for us to see that this is not a necessary corollary of our psychological, or our physiological, awareness. Nowadays we know quite well that we are " cousins of the ape "; but that does not make the thoughtful among us willing to reduce ourselves to apehood. Neither should our psychological self-awareness make us willing to abate our claim to moral responsibility. For there can be no question that we do feel responsible for our actions, unless we have consistently sought to destroy that sense in us; and even then, as countless incidents in real life testify, there is still left in us some trace of the moral sense, which troubles and disturbs us. Growth in true manhood, development toward genuine maturity, consists in our increasing capacity for moral discrimination; it carries with it the sharpening of what we call our conscience and the enhancing of our awareness that we are, in some genuine sense and degree, however limited this may be, responsible for ourselves as moral beings. Such development may be retarded; but it is childish to blame somebody else or something else for what is our own fault. I shall treat this problem at considerable length in a succeeding chapter.

It is not very important what *theory* we employ to explain the reality of human sin — the sinful situation and the sinful action. For myself, I have found that the treatment of this subject by the English writer to whom we have already referred, a writer now much criticized and usually entirely misunderstood, is most helpful. Dr. F. R. Tennant believed that it is through the insistent pressures that arise from a long-continued human misuse of our original instincts and habits that we have come to this state. These instincts and habits are good in themselves;

so far as man is concerned, they begin by being neutral in their effect. But when they are misused, abused, distorted, over a long period of time, they have consequences of a seriously deleterious kind. Furthermore, since as men we are social creatures, and our social belonging is not just an accident to our mankind but an integral part of it, the communication of these distortions is a consequence of our corporate existence. We cannot extricate ourselves from this social belonging, nor can we extricate ourselves from the corporate sin of man and its results. We must be delivered. But who shall deliver us? It is just here that we begin to see the meaning of the eighth of our statements about man: that in Jesus Christ this deliverance is accomplished.

7

Man Restored to His True Nature

Man is in defection from his true self — that was the seventh of the statements about man in our opening schema; the eighth follows directly upon it. Although man is in such defection, yet he has the potentiality of restoration to health or wholeness. In the language of Christian faith, he has been " saved " by being brought into a right relationship with his Creator and hence into a right relationship with himself and others. And this, which is a given fact for the Christian — a fact established in Jesus Christ — a man can be brought to accept and hence to *realize,* to enter into and find made actual, in his own life.

This is not all that the Christian would wish to say, however. For it is a precondition of such a conviction that Jesus Christ is not only the " Savior " who can thus restore man to wholeness; he is also the climactic point in the total God-man relationship, as it were " predestined " from " the foundation of the world." Despite the unhappy fact that many contemporary, popular Christian apologists and some reputable Christian theologians talk that way, it is not the general line of traditional Christian teaching that Jesus is "sent " to man only because God has decided to remedy the situation into which man has got himself, as if the coming of Jesus Christ were an afterthought in the divine purpose. On the contrary, and in

spite of the popular writing to which we have referred —
in which Christ becomes a sort of divine rescue expedition
to extricate man from his sad dilemma — the general line
of early Christian thought, and a persistent strain in the
succeeding ages of what might be called mainstream Christian theology, is that this event took place by God's " foreknowledge " and by the working out of his own plan for
his creation so far as man is concerned.

On the other hand, since we *are* in defection, since we
are estranged from our true destiny as man, it is almost inevitable that the act of God in Jesus Christ will strike us
preeminently in its " saving " quality. And it is here, in
our lostness, that the Christian faith for most of us comes
with its great affirmation. It not only says that God *will*
deliver us, through Christ; that is true, of course. It says
that *he has already done so,* through Christ. Now it is for
us to enter into, appropriate, accept, and realize that which
already has been done. By the human life that was God's
focal and decisive self-expression, his Word, *to* men and
for men and, above all, *in* man, something of supreme importance has happened; and it has happened *really* and
truly in the world of the God-man relationship and *not*
just as an idea in our heads. I shall say something more
about this in a moment. But what *has* happened? The answer is that what the Bible calls the " new creation," and
what Professor Tillich very aptly names " the new being in
Christ," has in actual and concrete fact been accomplished
in this world of experience. Things are not the same any-
more. God has done something; he " has set forth his Son
to be the expiation for our sins, and not ours only, but the
sins of the whole world." Some people appear to think
that the redemption of the world by the action of God in
Christ is chiefly what I might call an affair " in the mind "

— it is an idea that we accept because it is convincing to us and that, when accepted, then can become for us a belief we hold. But this sort of "mentalism" makes nonsense of the whole New Testament witness. The Bible says that God *already* has done something in Christ; and our job is to accept what he has done. Something has happened — Christ has been born, lived, taught, suffered, died, risen again. This something will not "come alive" in us unless we accept it, but it is *there* to be accepted. Acceptance is the work of faith, but the faith is in an event that is more than an event in our minds.

I wish to emphasize both sides of this, because I believe that there is considerable confusion and misunderstanding at this point. Jesus of Nazareth is a figure in history who was known as a Prophet and Master to his disciples and others. He was not *obviously* divine to those who knew him in the days of his flesh; he was a man among men, although a man of unusual quality and stupendous impact on others. Hence, to attempt to prove his divinity from some particular area of his historic human life is to pursue a false hope; there is *no* area of his historic human life where deity *as such* is to be found plain for all to see. In everything that he said and did he was a man; and a historian, looking at that life lived in Palestine, will say exactly what the companions of Jesus at the time would have said: here is a human life, great in its impact, wonderful in its quality, but human all the same. On the other hand, the faith that began with the disciples' initial dim insight and has continued and developed since their time up to the present day has penetrated into the mystery of this true human life of Jesus, lived at a given time in history, and has found there something more than humanity. God can be known only by faith, wherever he is known at all, and we only confuse and confound the matter if we think that in what Christians call the incarnate life, God is to be seen present and at work directly and immediately to our knowledge without any such faith on our part. Always, the way in which God is known, met, experienced in a living communion, is through the self-giving, the commitment, the surrender, the whole-lived trust, which is the meaning of faith. Precisely the same principle applies to the awareness of the presence and work of God in Christ. Only when with heart and mind and soul and will, with all our being, we give ourselves in complete response to our Lord's person and service, do we begin to know who he is.

For the Christian assertion about Jesus Christ is " very much more than a historical fact; it means a religious experience, an act of faith working upon a historical fact; and the product of the two is something which neither of them, taken separately, could ever have been. . . . The fact by itself cannot compel us to the judgment " that Jesus is truly divine as well as truly human or, in the language of the old formularies, which we may well wish to rephrase but which no faithful Christian would wish to deny, that he is " God as well as man." But it is equally true that " the religious experience, taken by itself, shares the same disability; for no amount of believing that something is true can actually make it so." We require both fact *and* faith.

I have been quoting from an Oxford theologian of the last generation, James Matthew Thompson, and I shall continue the quotation: " Suppose, now, that we take fact and faith, as we always find them in real life, together. Suppose that we give to each its utmost value: that we allow, as historical facts, historically provable, the extraordinary personal influence that Christ exercised over all who met him, sick or whole; the depth and directness of his insight into things human and divine; his personal holiness, and his burning enthusiasm; his unique self-sacrifice for love of sinners; and his intimate faith towards God; and suppose that we allow, as the proper work of religious experience and faith, just such an insight into and appreciation of this character of Christ as finds in it a supreme revelation of the nature of God, and as issues in prayer, and imitation, and worship, then shall we not be on our way to giving this doctrine of the divinity of our Lord the highest possible meaning, and one which both the progress of [Biblical] criticism and the growth of faith are likely to make more, and not less, secure? " [31]

Thompson is here saying that the actual historical fact, about which we read in the Gospels, can become for us only what in truth it really is — the Self-Expression of God for our wholeness — when we have surrendered to it and lived our lives, " in prayer, and imitation, and worship," in terms of it. The renewal, restoration, reintegration, whole-making, of human life — *from* its defection *to* its perfection — is a " live option " for us only as and when we respond to it. Yet it *has* happened, or else there would be nothing there to which we could respond. We have here a special and crucial case of the relationship of objective fact and subjective apprehension to which we referred in an earlier chapter; our interest at the moment, however, is simply to point out that both are necessary to the reality here in question: for Jesus Christ to be known for what in very truth he is, we must commit ourselves to him in faith. Otherwise he may remain an interesting historical figure; he will never accomplish in us that which the Christian centuries have declared that he is able to do.

Let me now quote another writer, this time William

Scott Palmer, who some forty years ago wrote these moving words: " If [a] man never opposed God, if he were always permeable to the divine [inflow], he would indeed
be manifestly God's Son, wholly his, living in his life,
making him . . . known in terms of man, as a man among
men. The manifestation of God in the man would and
must be local . . . in a place and at a stated time; God
[in the full reality of his being] would be, as always, in-
finitely beyond it, but he would be really present there,
he would be revealed in the man according to the measure
of man. . . . There God, embracing finitude and growing in wisdom and stature, would become at last ' manifest in the flesh ' . . . God, ever striving in each of us,
knocking always at the door of every heart, would also
draw near to us from without in a visible, intelligible sacrament, and by love eloquent in the actual life of one
man." [32]

The only critical comment that I should wish to make
about this fine passage is that it would have been better
to say that in Christ not only do we see a man's opening
himself to the " divine inflow " but also (and much more
significantly) we see God himself taking the initiative and
securing that the " opening " does indeed take place. God's
will and purpose of self-expression comes first — it always
does in every area of the God-man relationship. It pre-
pares and makes ready the way, so that " in the fullness of
the time," when all is " set " for the action, the combina-
tion of divine Self-Expression and human receptivity can
" clinch ": " The Word was made flesh, and dwelt among
us." But Palmer here has made the point which is, I
think, so important for us. Jesus Christ is not remote from
us, as if he were a visitant from another planet; he is one
of us, our Brother as well as our Lord. Yet in that very

oneness he is the actualization, the making real, the vivid and vital effecting in the concrete event of a truly human life, the genuine embodiment, of the truth about us as men. The difference between us and him, as Palmer says in another place, is " the difference between the unbroken whole and the more or less of imperfection in other men."

I quite realize that some theologians, if they read these words, will raise their eyebrows and say, " Aha, he speaks of difference only of degree but not of kind." To this I should answer, " Yes, but please drop the adverb ' only,' as if that kind of difference meant nothing at all." Difference of degree may still be enormous difference. The difference is between the sinful men who even in their sin are still made in God's image and in whom God dwells, *and* that One in whom God so lives and moves and works that he is nothing other than God's express Image in man. My purpose in stressing this is not to be theologically controversial but to guarantee what I am convinced is of crucial importance. Christ is *both* our Brother *and* our Lord; and God in him speaks to the never-destroyed image in us; our sin has not reduced to nothing our relationship to God, however seriously, tragically, terribly it has damaged it; and our theology of redemption is not, as one of my friends has put it, a " desperation-theology " but is rather a theology of restoration.

In our thinking about Christ we must build upon a view of God and man and the world, and their interrelationship, which is grounded in the realities with which men are inescapably confronted; realities that we know in the depths of our experience, on the one hand, and that we apprehend and then interpret through an act of faith, of self-giving, of commitment, on the other. In our situation as men, here and now, it is inevitable that we shall get at

the Christian faith through the forgiveness of sin, through
the empowering given us for the life in grace, that is, the
divine favor and acceptance and its working out in us. We
must remember, however, that forgiveness is never simply
retrospective. It is not only a looking back and saying that
the wrong-doing and wrong-thinking and wrong-speaking
of which we are guilty, and which we would undo, are
overcome by the goodwill of God toward us, so that our
past is blotted out. Forgiveness is prospective; it looks to
the future. It is to be understood as God's taking us into
his companionship, making us his " fellow workers " as
Paul has it, binding us to himself for the days to come and
for all eternity. Somebody has said that the Christian doctrine of the forgiveness of sin and renewal of life, stated in
the classical Biblical phrase as " justification by faith," is
the affirmation that God takes us here and now for what
we are, yet also takes us for what we may and can become
through his help. That way of stating it rightly emphasizes
the ongoing process of Christian life.

We ought not to let ourselves get bogged down in our
recognition of the sinfulness — the defection or estrangement, the " incurvation on self " — of which we are so
painfully aware when we are honest with ourselves. If we
put *all* our attention on this sinfulness, we may forget the
great affirmation of Christian faith which is much more
important than anything about our mean little selves. For
the strong Christian insistence on Jesus Christ as the decisive and adequate Self-Expression of God in genuinely
human terms, the Express Image of God in man, should
make plain to us that our own tiny God-given possibilities
and potentialities, and our own meager realizations of
God's will and way and presence in us, despite our sinful
situation and sinful actions, are real and good and true

and wonderful, so far as they go. Christian faith declares to us that the Lord whom we serve is that One in whom all this which we know and cherish and which we should never deny or distrust is brought to what I have called " actualization " — completed accomplishment and realization. The Man of Nazareth is the Savior who is the living Christ of our contemporary companioning. But he is not the denial of what we *really* are; he is the fulfillment of it. Far too many present-day theologians forget this or reject it out of hand; in consequence, their whole view of Christianity is sadly impoverished and, in my judgment, distorted and wrong.

Dorothy M. Emmet, the English philosopher, has written in a recent book of " the increased vitality which comes from release from anxiety and self-consciousness through loving absorption in the task in hand, or *in the person before you*" (italics mine), and she goes on to say that " religion, when purified of fear and obsessive elements, has to do (among other things) with the awakening and sustaining of this power." [33] Here we have a superb description of what in part it means " to be saved " — to be " set right " and to be " given grace " by and in the community which is fellowship with the Lord Jesus Christ, historic person and risen Lord of the Christian church. But this must be taken into oneself, made one's own, to be effectual in one's life. As Dr. Robert H. Bonthius points out in his stimulating book *Christian Paths to Self-Acceptance*,[34] the basic precondition of genuine self-acceptance is accepting the fact that one has been accepted. Dr. Paul Tillich has argued rightly that in fact this is nothing other than the true meaning of " justification by faith." This is but a way of saying that the fulfillment of human life, the restoration of our humanity to its divinely intended norm, the recovery of it from estrangement from self, from others, and from God, is not something that we can do in and of ourselves, " under our own steam," so to say. It comes to us when we lose ourselves and when we are willing to lose ourselves; in fact, it comes to us when we fall in love.

Now I know how dangerous this kind of talk can be. But I see no way out of saying it. I pointed out in discussing sexuality in man that true love is a giving of self in answer or response to a self that gives — love is the gift of self to the gift of self. Human love, when it is deep and real, is *always* of grace, never of works. Nobody can " work himself up " into a state of true love; as the phrase goes, " we *fall* in love." It *happens* to us; we do not achieve it. This, which we all know to be true of the common human experience of love as distinguished from the distortion of lust, has its supreme illustration in our saving relationship with God. For it is of the very essence of Christian faith, when one is speaking of man's sin, to affirm that " God set forth his Son to be the expiation for our sins." That is, God acted first. He loved *before* we loved: " We love him, because he first loved us," says the writer of The First Letter of John. It is when we are grasped by, caught up into, persuaded to surrender to, the love of God manifest in Jesus Christ, that we come to the fulfillment of human personality which is promised to us. It is not our achievement, through our own effort, although plenty of effort is required of us; it is first and foremost a gift, which we accept as it is offered to us, and which we then work out in the daily experience of life.

Of course the fulfillment is not realized all at once; and often one of our difficulties is that we tend to think that it is. But it *takes time;* there is so much that is twisted and distorted in us, as we know ourselves, that it cannot be done in an instant. That is why Christian life is normally a process of growth and not the sudden transformation which some popular evangelists would suggest. We are to " grow in grace, and in the knowledge of our Lord and Saviour Jesus Christ." Here is where the " means of grace " — the proclamation of the Word from the pulpit, the receiving of the sacrament of Holy Communion, the reading of the Scriptures, prayer, and meditation — have their necessary place in the Christian life. Here, too, is where the fellowship of all faithful people comes to our aid. We are not alone; we are surrounded by a great " cloud of witnesses "; we are members of the Christian community and not isolated and insulated from the strong currents of life in Christ which flow down the centuries from the days of his flesh in Palestine.

In the fact of our being men, a common God-man relationship is given and established. To speak in a parable, it is the carbon that we all share. But in us the carbon remains but charcoal. In Christ, we dare assert, there is the Diamond. Gerard Manley Hopkins once referred to Christ as " immortal diamond," and he went on to say that we too are to become " diamond," and although he makes it too instantaneous for common Christian experience, he sees that we can become such only through him who *is* " immortal diamond ":

> In a flash, at a trumpet crash,
> I am all at once what Christ is, since he was what I am, and
> This Jack, joke, poor potsherd, patch, matchwood, immortal diamond,
> Is immortal diamond.
> *(That Nature Is a Heraclitean Fire and of the comfort of the Resurrection)* [35]

That is a picturesque way of putting what Prof. Alfred Edward Taylor stated in more prosaic words. In *The Faith of a Moralist,* Taylor wrote that if men are to see the true significance of their human existence and acquire the power to be what in fact they are in God's intention, they need " a life which is at once everywhere creaturely and yet also everywhere more than creaturely, because its limitations, circumscriptions, and infirmities, whatever they may be, interpose no obstacle to the divine and eternal purpose which controls and shines through it, but are themselves vehicles of that purpose." [36] That there has been such a life, and that it is the life of Jesus Christ, is (as Professor Taylor goes on to say) the " undemonstrated and indemonstrable " conviction of the Christian centuries. This is a long and complicated, but, I think, a thoroughly satisfactory, way of saying that for their true fulfillment men need to encounter One who is as human as they are, but at the same time as divine as God is — what is required is the presence of One in whom human life, the human life which we all have to live here and now in this world, is the living instrument (in Athanasius' fine word, *organon*) for the Word of God, for God in his Self-Expression manward and in man. Or, to put it in yet another way, the fulfillment of human life demands that the Self-Expression of God in and toward mankind be focused, concentrated, intensified, decisively manifest, in One of our own kind. Only so can that Self-Expression really touch us and make us what we are meant to be. This assertion about Jesus Christ is indeed as Taylor says " the conviction which gives the Christian religion its specific character."

But *who* are to be " saved " or fulfilled? A select few? Or is the promise made for all men? Is " salvation " limited or universal? These are the questions with which we must now deal.

"For us men, and for our salvation . . ." So the statement runs in the so-called Nicene Creed, the ancient confession of faith from the fourth and fifth centuries of the Christian era. It states succinctly the agreed conviction of all Christians, at all times and in all places, that the Lord Jesus Christ was born among us, lived humanly with us, died the death which we all must die, and was victorious over death, and that as a result those whom he did not refuse to call his brethren receive what the Christian centuries have described as "salvation." But what is meant by this last word? How should we interpret it? This is the question with which we are immediately concerned. Since the term "salvation" has a long history and is rooted in the Biblical writings, a brief explanation of the meaning it has borne in Scripture is in order. The Hebrew conception of salvation has its roots in the idea of widening, expanding, and developing, and it came to signify victory over enemies. Since God ultimately gives all victory, he is appropriately described as "Savior," and hence it is God's deliverance of men that is rightly denoted by the word "salvation." In the Old Testament this idea comes finally (as in Deutero-Isaiah) to mean the victory of the righteous God over all that would oppress his people, while in the Suffering Servant poems, included in the material found in Deutero-Isaiah, this salvation involves suffering on the part of the one who is God's agent in obtaining this deliverance.

In the New Testament these basic ideas are carried over, but subtly modified (as are all Old Testament conceptions) in the light of the Self-Expression of God in his incarnate Son Jesus Christ. Generally speaking, salvation in the New Testament means deliverance by Christ from a variety of evils, enemies, ills — a salvation granted now to those who in faith respond to the grace of God in the incarnate Lord, but a salvation that is also to be consummated in " the great day " when God brings his whole creation to its completion.

Etymologically, as we have seen, the word " salvation " itself is cognate with a whole series of terms, both Greek and Latin, which suggest wholeness, health, fullness of life, and the like — the notion being that deliverance from evils brings wholeness and health. There are other Christian terms that have a close relationship to " salvation " and that should at least be mentioned here: e.g., redemption, reconciliation, atonement. The first, " redemption," from its Biblical usage suggests the buying back by the owner of one who has been in bondage or slavery, and hence means " making free "; " reconciliation " implies that " enmity " or loss of friendship and communion is overcome and an open relationship established between those who were alienated or estranged; while " atonement," the compendious word commonly used in discussion of the work of Christ, means in its final sense the bringing together of those who had been separated, the restoration of proper unity through the establishment of the conditions that remove both the causes and the consequences of division.

Despite the apparent similarity of these and many other terms in Christian usage, there are some important distinctions that ought to be made. In the developed Christian sense of the word, salvation suggests the forgiveness of sins, through which by God's free pardon those who have offended against him and his holy will are treated as if they were already what by grace they may become —

namely, sons of God, living in filial obedience to their Heavenly Father. But it can also suggest the righting of evil conditions, the destruction of inimical powers, the conquest of " all that is wrong in the world " — in a word, the overcoming of evil. Again, it can suggest the ultimate restoration of all creation to its original intention in the purpose of God, to which we look forward when, like Mother Julian of Norwich, we say that " all shall be well, all manner of thing shall be well." [37] Finally, in the widest sense (and a sense that is often found in modern theology) salvation can mean the total effect of the work of Christ, his " benefits " for men, whatever they may be.

It is my own belief that the last of these possible meanings is not only all-inclusive but is also a better clue to the whole significance of that which our Lord did and does for men, as well as all that his coming reveals and effects in the total structure of reality. Furthermore, I am convinced that the inevitable emphasis which sinful men must give to the truth that through Christ they know forgiveness and reconciliation, has sometimes been exaggerated to mean *all* that could be said about Christ's mission in the world. Hence we find theologies that are so centered on the fact of sin that the glory of God's grace becomes a kind of corollary to sin; and we are not unfamiliar with the teaching that had men not sinned, Christ would not have come to dwell among us because he need not have done so.

Indeed, the last of these views (commonly called Thomist because Thomas Aquinas finally came down for the teaching that the incarnation was primarily " remedy " for sin) is thought by many to be the only possible Christian view. But already I have urged that this forgets the whole stream of Christian teaching that is commonly called Scotist (since Duns Scotus was its outstanding medieval advocate) , and in which it is asserted that even had man *not* sinned, the incarnation would yet have taken place, for it is God's ultimate purpose to unite his creation with himself as intimately as possible while maintaining its integrity *as* creation, and that so far as men are concerned the central action that both states and effects this is the life of the incarnate Word. It is, of course, obvious enough that this view is in one sense theoretical, since, as a matter of fact, man has sinned and does sin. But the point that Duns Scotus, and others who like myself share this view, would wish to make can still be defended, since it is difficult to see how otherwise one can regard the incarnation as other than an afterthought of God, even if one does not succumb to the notion that in his foreknowledge God both knew (and willed? the *horribile decretum*) man's sin and so provided the remedy for a selected few.

As can readily be seen, the specific problem here posed opens up a wide field of theological discussion. And a discussion so short as this is not the place to pursue these ramifications; it must suffice to have put the problem, and then to go on to outline, as briefly as possible, the view of salvation which seems to be most satisfactory in respect to the question: *Who* is saved?

In the first place, I have argued throughout this book that we are at liberty to " demythologize " (if that is the right word in this context) the Biblical view and relate it closely to the etymological background of the words by centering our attention on the ideas of health, wholeness, free and abundant life. For basic to the notion of deliverance, surely, is the presence of that which establishes the free and full life for which man and the society to which he belongs were intended by God. Here we are greatly helped on the theological side by the work of such men as

Paul Tillich, and the many religious thinkers who are emphasizing so strongly the close connection between religion and health, and also from the medical, psychiatric, and psychoanalytical disciplines, by the work of those who are beginning to recognize that ultimate orientation, supreme faith, and the attitudes that follow from this are essential to the total well-being of their patients. So in our time, as Professor Tillich has noted, one of the most meaningful images for Christ as Savior is the one that portrays him as the Healer, both of men's bodies and of their " souls " (their minds, their emotional life, etc.) .

Secondly, we must learn to extend the notion of salvation to include *all* that comes to men from *all* sources and by *all* channels to bring about their restoration to their true (i.e., God-intended) nature. Just as there is no knowledge that is *exclusively* " saving knowledge," although there *is* knowledge that in *special and distinctive ways* thus operates, so there is no narrow channel of salvation, although there are particularly appropriate and peculiarly effective channels. In this way we can broaden our base while at the same time we are free to maintain (as a Christian must maintain) that there is indeed something special and distinctive about what a man in faith receives by God's grace through the agency of Jesus Christ. Nor is this an unheard-of idea in Christian circles. For the great theologians have always sought to find ways of preserving both of these emphases, whether it has been by the concepts of " common grace " or of " uncovenanted mercies " or of " latent operation of the Word of God " or by the wider insistence, found notably in the patristic period, on the Logos as both *spermatikos* (in all men) and *ensarkos* (or specially incarnate or " enfleshed " or " enmanned ") in Jesus Christ.

In the third place, a corollary of the Christian doctrine of God as all-sovereign love (which is what the creedal phrase " God the Father Almighty " signifies) is that all men shall be saved, and that God's will is in the long run bound to accomplish that for which it sets out — there will be no " pockets of resistance " left, when God has accomplished his final victory over sin, evil, and death. How to hold this universalist doctrine without destroying man's sense of moral responsibility is another question; but I should suggest that Karl Barth, for one, and J. A. T. Robinson (whose little book *In the End, God* [38] deserves wider reading and study than thus far it has received), for another, have pointed the way by their teaching on the election of the whole race in Christ and by their insistence that God's loving Self-Expression is so subtle and so persuasive that all men, and the whole creation, will be won (*not* coerced) into a response to the Creator, so that " God may be all in all." Anything less would seem a blasphemous denial of the central reality of the Christian revelation — " God is love " — and would imply the setting up, in the place of the God and Father of our Lord Jesus Christ, of a heathen idol who ought not to be worshiped but destroyed.

Fourthly, we need not worry ourselves unduly about whatever rational and moral creatures there may be in " other worlds." The God who in Christ has spoken savingly to men doubtless has his ways of reaching the secret heart of whatever rational and moral creatures may inhabit other planets. Indeed, if he *is* the God and Father of our Lord Jesus Christ, we may be confident that he has done, is doing, and will do precisely this. Once again, the doctrine of God is at stake here, and sometimes one is compelled to think that many who profess and call themselves Christians believe intellectually in a God who is horribly sub-Christian.

But, it may be asked, what does all this say about the

Christian mission to the world? Simply this: it is *beneath the level of Christian faith* to speak of our commending Christianity to others on the ground that without accepting that faith they are doomed to perish everlastingly. It *is* the consequence of Christian faith to seek by every legitimate means, in season and out of season, to bring others to the place where they can share with us that which is the heart of our own being — the love of God revealed and active in Jesus Christ, through whom we have known so rich and full a life that it is unthinkable that we should not wish others to know it too. Christians ought to stop thinking of themselves as being the " saved " and ought rather to think of themselves as those who as " fellow workers " with God are seeking, by his grace empowering them, to bring to all men everywhere the life with him, through Christ, which he has been pleased, through no merit of our own, to permit us to enjoy. Canon Leonard Hodgson, recently Regius Professor of Divinity at Oxford, has spoken again and again in book after book (most recently in his Gifford Lectures *For Faith and Freedom*) [39] of the terrible apostasy of the church in this respect. And he has said that it may be that the Holy Spirit is leading us into a rediscovery in this age of the profound truth that we are indeed " saviors," not by any right of our own or through any power of our own but precisely because we are Christ's people and as such are called to do Christ's work in the world.

In this all too brief answer to the question, *Who is saved?* perhaps I have raised more questions than I have answered. But I think that this points to an enormous item of unfinished business on the church's theological (not to say pastoral) agenda. Have we really, seriously, earnestly, wrestled with what it means to believe that the ultimate ground of being, the determiner of all destiny, the Lord of heaven and earth, is nothing other than the all-sovereign love which in Jesus Christ, for us men and for our wholeness, was incarnate among us, lived with us, died in order that we might share his life, and lives evermore as the guarantee of the reality of that which he came to reveal and to do?

8

Man Made for Eternity

We began by talking about who man is and what he is here for, and we have seen him in his creaturely dependence and in his drive toward fulfillment in God; we have seen him as living in community with his brethren and as an embodied or amphibious being; we have seen, too, his defection from true manhood. Everything about him points toward full self-realization, but alas! he is not able to make this actual in his own life. We have seen his estrangement from God, and hence his self-alienation as well as his separation from his fellowmen with whom nonetheless he is inescapably bound up in a " bundle of life." But we have also seen that this is not the whole story, for the Christian faith, " undemonstrated and indemonstrable " — and for that very reason a challenge to self-commitment, " engagement," surrender — has told us that in the Man Christ Jesus, God has changed this picture. He has crowned our human potentiality by the Actuality of his own Self-Expression in a Man; and he has wrought atonement, at-one-ment, so that by participation in the life of that same Man, we are integrated, made one, brought back to ourselves, to others, and to God. We are, in fact, put in the way of being fulfilled. So we may become what already in God's purpose we are: sons of God and heirs of his (that is to say, of eternal) life. In union with the Lord Jesus Christ in faith, by prayer and communion, by acquaintance with him in Holy Scripture, and by seeking to follow " the blessed steps of his most holy life," we may grow in grace toward that true fulfillment, more and more coming to see the purpose God has for us, more and more finding ourselves enabled to accomplish that purpose, more and more becoming " en-Christed " men.

But not completely in this present life — which brings us to the ninth of our points about human nature. For man is mortal; he is the being who is going to die and who knows that he is going to die. This knowledge differentiates him from the animals who indeed are going to die also, but who do not have to face this fact consciously and with the certainty of their mortality ever before them. Improvement in medical care, bettering of social conditions, all that is now being done or that can be done to make life happier, more comfortable, and more secure, will never cancel out the fact that the mortality rate remains exactly 100 percent of the population. To live with this fact is a condition of healthy human existence; to deny it, or to attempt to live as if it were not true, is both silly and dishonest. I do not mean to suggest, of course, that a man should spend all or most of his time contemplating his coming death; that would also be silly, although at least it would not be dishonest. But I do intend to suggest that there was more truth than we have often been ready to allow in the admonition so frequently given by our ancestors that we must " prepare for death." And the attempt to deny death's harsh reality by the devices made popular by American funerary customs is an unworthy evasion of truth — unworthy because it really reduces men to an animal level, even and perhaps chiefly when it expresses itself through a " prettying up " of the terrible truth.

Now, Christianity has never denied the fact of death. But for Christianity that fact is not the whole story, since Christian faith includes also the affirmation that " God has prepared for them that love him such good things as pass man's understanding." The Christian view of human nature has therefore always included a note of " otherworldliness " — not, mind you, of *next*-worldliness, in which we may seek to put off to another world what it is our duty to do in this one. But *other*worldliness, by which I mean here the awareness of the eternal realm that surrounds this one and that penetrates it, as the poet says, with " bright shoots of everlastingness," is integral to Christian faith and at the same time is highly relevant to the Christian understanding of what it means to be a man.

It is in this present existence, indeed, that we begin to move toward our fulfillment in God, if we surrender ourselves, souls and bodies, to the love of God and the accomplishing of his holy will. Even now, so the Christian dares to say, man may live, in part, in heavenly places; even now he may share, in part, the vision of God; even now, in " earnest " (*arrabōn* is Paul's word) the Kingdom of God is present among us. Here already we have a foretaste of that complete fulfillment of human nature which is man's highest destiny and God's purpose for him. This, I take it, is what in the last analysis the concept of " salvation " is all about.

Begun here, but to be accomplished in the life which is not so much beyond as through and in spite of, yet also given in, the fact of our mortality. For, as we have seen, God, who created and still creates us in the here and now, can and will re-create and re-constitute our manhood in its integrity out of the ruins of that manhood in the death which is inescapably before us. Of this the victory of Christ over death assures us. Opinions may differ as to how this occurs, and they certainly do differ in respect to what we somewhat stupidly call the " conditions " of life after death; but the American *Book of Common Prayer,* when it speaks of " continual growth " in God's love and service, and at the same time insists that we are still united with the departed in that one bundle of life which now is known as " the communion of saints," gives us a sufficient working faith on these matters. Man's end is not here in this world, although this world marks the end of our this-worldly existence. Beyond this world there is the perfect fulfillment in what we call heaven; and of this Augustine, at the end of *The City of God,* has said what is perhaps the last word in any literature apart from Scripture itself: " There we shall rest and see, see and love, love and praise. This is what shall be in the end without end. For what other end do we propose to ourselves than to attain to the Kingdom of God of which there is no end? " [40]

Yet there are some who will say that all this is simply " pie in the sky " thinking, to use the phrase popularized years ago by one of the early American labor movements. But is it? Perhaps we should spend a little more time in considering this Christian conviction about man's destiny.

" I am a stranger here, heaven is my home." So ran the old hymn, now so much condemned. Unquestionably a great deal of next-worldliness, as we have called it, has been found among Christians in past ages. It is possible so to overemphasize the hope of heaven that the responsibilities as well as the values of this present world are seriously minimized, and our days in the here and now, if not denied attention, at any rate are reduced to the level of a mere vestibule to " the other life " which is thought to be the only important part of the picture. On the other hand, it is possible so to forget or minimize the reality of the Christian hope of heaven that attention, interest, and thought are centered on this immediate world alone; and the result of such total concentration on this-worldliness is likely to be a futile secularism in which the present sphere of life soon loses the tang and flavor that attach to it when it is seen and appreciated as shot through with the eternal reality of some " Kingdom not of this world." Such a futile secularism is no better, surely, than a sterile supernaturalism. Common sense would seem to indicate that it is only when concern for this world and its ways is balanced by the recognition that man's destiny and consummation are beyond this world, that we can have a healthy and sound state of affairs. Only when a keen sense of the circumambient reality of the eternity to which in the end we belong is balanced by vital action in the mundane world in which we now live do we have a just and ordinate sense of the meaning of human life.

Nowadays, of course, the tendency is all in the direction of a semispiritualized secularism. Indeed, this is one of the reasons that a good deal of contemporary religious thinking is so much out of tune with the traditional thought of the Christian church. It does not take much acquaintance-ship with the historic liturgies of the church, its offices of prayer, and its public services of worship, nor much knowledge of the writings of the great saints and theologians of the Christian past, to see that their entire outlook was governed by the dominant theme of man's heavenly destiny, the conviction that in at least some sense heaven *is* my home, and the hope of human fulfillment beyond this world of space and time. Actually " hope " is far too weak a word to use here. There was a strong expectation, involving certainty and conviction, in this perennial Christian conception that gave it an overmastering influence on all life and experience. Every moment of every day, every bit of human thought, and every area of human action was modified and colored by a deep sense of the more-than-worldly. So much have we lost this vivid sense of the reality of eternal life and the imminence (and I do *not* mean " immanence ") of the eternal world, that it is not surprising to hear, as one did recently, that at a series of meetings of a great commission of American religious leaders, called to discuss important issues of Christian faith, it was impossible to get more than one or two of the members to go beyond a rather vague assent to the statement that " the souls of the righteous are in the hand of God," when it was desired to make some clear definition of the Christian faith in eternal life.

Certainly we must allow that such a reticence has a certain value. The attempt to draw accurate maps of the " other world " is bound to fail; the best we can ever hope to do in that direction is to offer suggestions, intimations, hints, about the state and quality of life beyond this one. The traditional pictorial representations of heaven, like those of purgatory and hell, are at best to be taken symbolically rather than literally. But it is certainly a grievous state of affairs when, on the one hand, the Christian is urged to have as part of his faith the conviction of " immortality," while, on the other hand, he is yet expected to hold it as in itself and at best a vague uncertainty with little influence on life. It reminds one of the lines composed by an Oxford don:

> O let us never, never doubt
> What nobody is sure about.

How to restore something of the keen sense of the reality of eternal life to the jaded modern mind presents us with a most difficult and stubborn problem. But surely one of the first things to be done is to get out of our thinking, as quickly as we can, the notion that eternal life is merely a future state. The phrase " the afterlife " has done a considerable amount of harm, because it is taken to imply that everything relating to eternity comes *after* this life in a strictly temporal sense. Yet in our day-by-day experience, ever surrounding us, penetrating our created world and our creaturely activity within that world, giving its own unique tang to all that we do and know, is the eternal reality of life in God.

Henry Vaughan's phrase, " bright shoots of everlastingness," which we have quoted before in this chapter, tells us of the constant entrance of eternity into our lives. The sense of heightened meaning, the joys of enduring comradeship, the recognition of beauty, a momentary glimpse of true goodness: here we have traces of heaven. " Little bits of heaven " are continually to be found in this world; eternity is not all future, but indeed largely a matter of present, living experience.

Another fact that can help us here is the recognition that even the most secular existence is never without some disturbing awareness of the more-than-earthly. We remember how it is remarked in Browning's *Bishop Blougram's Apology* that it is precisely when everything seems secularly ordered and explained, and when therefore the world has been made safe for secularity alone:

> Just when we're safest
> There's a sunset touch, a fancy from a flower-bell,
> Someone's death, a chorus-ending from Euripides,

> And that's enough for fifty doubts and fears,
> As old and yet as new as nature's self,
> To enter in . . .[41]

There do come to us those moments when the "prison walls" of this-worldly existence are shattered, even if this occurs to our own annoyance or disturbance. Most of us like most of the time to be "cabined, cribbed, confined" in a neat little this-world existence; and then there come upon us the moments when heaven breaks in upon us, when ultimate realities speak to us under many and strange incognitos, when in our immediate present there is some inexorable demand or some inexplicable succor.

I said, "when heaven breaks in." I might almost as well have said, "when hell breaks in," for the truth is that the sense of the impingement or insertion of eternity into time can bring vividly before us the awful possibility of a futile, hopeless, frustrated destiny, just as it can bring the bright prospect of a fulfillment of life in the presence and by the power of the eternal God. When men see deepest into their own lives here and now and grasp their underlying significance and their "grounding," they see the height to which life is called as well as the depths to which it is capable of sinking. Both heaven and hell are real elements in our experience, if once we get into the habit of living like men, rather than existing as highly developed simians who happens to possess certain rational powers.

It is amazing to see how the realization of eternal issues dominates the great literatures of the world. Shakespeare is an obvious illustration; but he is influenced by Christianity and so may be thought to be prejudiced. But the Greek tragedians show the same understanding. Lately I devoted an entire summer to a rereading of Aeschylus, Sophocles, and Euripides; and the one thing that struck me above all else was the vast cosmic sweep of their thinking, the sharpness of their moral insight in the light of that cosmic stretch, and the way in which human life, in the immediacy of the here and now, was taken to be related to the ultimacies of right and wrong, good and evil, eternal hope and everlasting despair. Their characters live and move and have their being in this world, but it is against a cosmic background and in a cosmic frame of reference. This is the understanding which we must recover for our generation. It is necessary to our healthy human living that we see our lives, not to speak of the lives of those whom we hold dear, against a cosmic background and in a cosmic frame of reference. Only that awareness will lift us and them above triviality and cheapness, and give our lives and the lives of other men a dignity and beauty that are imperishable. Then we shall be able to see that for men such as this, Lawrence Binyon spoke wisely when he affirmed that " time shall not wither them, nor the years condemn." That is the insight necessary on the path to understanding the real meaning of human fulfillment in God.

If this is hard to express, it is not because it is untrue but because our human apprehension is so weak and our human understanding so feeble. Christians so often appropriate far too little of the riches of their faith in this respect; they comprehend so little of what they do in fact claim to believe. But for all of us who even in some tiny way have grasped a bit of the meaning of Christian discipleship, there is truth in the old song, imperfect and inadequate as it is: " I am a stranger here, heaven is my home." The truth, if it is put more satisfactorily although more prosaically, is that our ultimate destiny, our highest realization, and our complete fulfillment are beyond all that this world can offer or contain. We men are pilgrims, indeed, who are set in this world to make it a fit colony for the sons of God, but there is also a sense in which we are resident aliens who can never forget the homeland.

In *The Aeneid,* Vergil has the moving picture of Anchises and the other dead, standing by the river that separated them from the eternal habitations, and " stretching out hands with longing toward the farther shore." This yearning for more than is now known and seen is part of what Christians mean by " the hope of heaven." And Søren Kierkegaard, concluding his apologia entitled *The Point of View for My Work as an Author,* says that of himself one day it will be written that from the historical perspective " he died of a mortal disease, but poetically speaking he died of a longing for eternity, where his happiness will be to give thanks everlastingly to the God who brought him on his way." [42] That is the adequate, as it is the Christian, phrasing of what we mean when we say that " heaven is our home," and when we dare to assert that complete fulfillment of human life and the satisfaction of man's drive for God, can be had only in the never-failing presence of God himself, in the communion of saints. And it is a legitimate hope, in the deepest sense of that word, that this will not finally be denied to any man.

9

Man as Created Freedom

We turn now to the tenth and last of the assertions about man with which we have been concerned in this book: man is a free being, not an automaton or a machine, and in his freedom he is able to make choices and hence to act with moral responsibility.

Before we begin our discussion, however, it will be useful to say something about the world in which men live, the world that is their given environment. Such an investigation will provide the context in which a consideration of human freedom will be most fruitful. For if the world itself is but a machine, man's freedom in it will be nugatory, while if the world has some " openness," so to say, human freedom will be a more rational and expected thing. What sort of world is this, then? Is it a mechanism that goes on in a routine fashion like a clock, or does it exhibit something of the character of a living organism? Were the Deists right in thinking that the creation is like a machine that once upon a time was set in operation by the divine Creator and now is left to run by itself? Or are those Christians, who by some odd accident have taken over what is essentially a Deistic view of the world, and who assume that view to be the orthodox one, right when they say that while the world of nature is indeed a machinelike affair, there are times when the Creator intrudes into or interferes with it, making repairs when it gets " out of order " or when it has been damaged by wear and tear? Or is the world but another name for whatever divine reality there is, so that Spinoza's phrase *deus sive natura* (God or otherwise nature) may be accepted in its obvious and face meaning? — which, incidentally, is not at all the meaning that the " God-intoxicated Jew " intended when he first used the phrase.

I believe that we can show that none of these positions is correct; that none of them corresponds to the facts that we know about the world; that none of them is adequate to the environment in which men are set and with which they must deal. Above all, the second view, which I have attributed to certain Christian thinkers, is not only inaccurate as a description of the facts but is very far indeed from the Biblical picture of the world, however popular that view may be with some who pride themselves on their very special orthodoxy. Let us then consider the two basic factors important to us as Christians: (1) what our observation of the world tells us and (2) what the Jewish-Christian Scriptures regard as the relationship between the world and God.

As to the first, we must turn to scientific study and the metaphysical orientation which that suggests. In contemporary science, the old-fashioned naturalism that was once fairly widely accepted has been dismissed by a very large number of those persons who work in the various scientific fields. The world is seen no longer as a simple unfolding of what was already present in it or as the reshuffling of a pack of old cards. The wide acceptance of the evolutionary point of view has made possible an allowance for epigenesis — the emergence of the genuinely new.

Hence the "higher levels" in the creation are not regarded as mere resultants of what has gone before but rather as the appearance in the total system of that which hitherto has not been known. So living matter, while it is contiguous with inanimate matter, yet possesses new characteristics that are special to its own particular way of ordering its components. This particular ordering is a genuine novelty in the evolutionary process and brings with it qualities, modes of behavior, distinctive reactions, that do not exist where that particular kind of ordering has not appeared. The general line taken by modern men of science, and by those who like Professor Whitehead and others have sought to draw out the metaphysical implications of scientific inquiry into the facts, is that the world is no dead automaton but rather an "organismic" reality, in which there is both continuity of process and the emergence of genuine novelty — new things do appear and must be reckoned with in any adequate account of the world. Thus living matter is different from inanimate matter; consciousness is not the same as life; the recognition of values and aspiration for their attainment are more than mere psychological functioning.

That is to say, modern science is much more acutely aware of the variety in the world, much more open to the distinctions within it, much more insistent on the possibility of the new appearing there, than the layman in scientific matters is likely to think. There is a cultural lag between the work of the foremost scientists and philosophers of science, and the "camp followers" of science, and an even greater gap exists between such men and the general public; it is important that we should recognize this, since we ought not to attack as "scientific thought" what is only the naïve reaction of popularizers as well as some of the scientific pioneers a hundred years ago, when the first attempts were made to work out a view of the world on the basis of scientific inquiry and experiment.

At the same time, an increasing number of thinkers who have used the findings of science in their effort to develop a philosophical interpretation of the world as a whole — a metaphysic, in brief — are prepared to admit that while the universe permits of increasingly precise *description* through scientific procedures, it cannot be *explained* by these methods. The world which science describes is contingent, changing, a world of phenomena; it neither explains itself nor does it of itself provide an answer to the deepest questions men are impelled to ask — questions concerning ultimate meaning, purpose, value, and intention. Hence there is a much greater readiness to listen to what may be said from the nonscientific side about a divine ground of existence, a reality in relation to which change occurs, a purpose that is being realized in the created order. The religious question is once again being asked; and the possibility of a religious answer is not entirely rejected.

What, then, do the Jewish-Christian Scriptures have to say on the relationship between God, understood as the ultimate explanation of all things and the purposer who works through them toward a goal, and the order of creation including nature, history, and human experience?

First, of course, the Scriptures are insistent on the reality of God and the necessity for his existence as explanation of all that is not God. The men who wrote the Scriptures did not think in scientific or philosophical idiom; they were more like poets, thinking in vivid pictorial images. But it requires no demonstration that they were convinced that " in the beginning God created the heaven and the earth "; that he upholds them " by the word of his power "; that he is ceaselessly their source and their governor. In the second place, the Scriptures do not regard the world as " apart from " God. They never fall into the Deistic position that the creation is unrelated to God save as he is the " first cause " of it. On the contrary, God is regarded as unfailingly active not only in sustaining the creation in existence but also in working in and through that creation, molding it to the ends he has determined. Never does he let it get out of his control; he is ceaselessly operative in every nook and cranny of the created world. It is remarkable — although some modern theologians forget this — that the Bible sees God always *in relation* to the world he made and is making; it does not speak of some " unmoved mover " dwelling in supreme isolation away from his creation. He is indeed " exalted far above all worlds," but this is only a metaphorical way of stating that he is never exhausted in his nature by the " operation of his hands." He is transcendent over his world, yes, but he is also unfailingly concomitant with and immanent in the world. This is to use philosophical language, which the Scriptures do not employ, to describe the consistent Biblical conviction that the " high and lofty One that inhabiteth eternity " is close at hand and at work in creation and that of every atom of creation it can be said that *because* God is there, " not one faileth." Thirdly, since God is faithful and consistent in his operation, his purpose runs throughout the creation; he is not a God who alters that purpose by whim or a change of mind. He can be counted on to act in the present and in the future in ways which are known from the past. This is not to suggest that he does not bring new things to pass, for certainly the Bible says that he does do this, but that there is a grand unity both in his plan and in the achievement of it which makes it possible for men to trust him and to rest upon his never-failing faithfulness to his revealed character and his established methods. That confidence, by the way, explains why the Old Testament is bound up with the New Testament in the Christian Bible.

The notion that God has created a world which is so badly constructed that it gets out of hand, that in consequence he must interfere or interpose or intrude to violate its great consistencies, and that he is not known by us excepting through such meddling, is a shocking denial of these three main Biblical emphases: that God is ultimately the one and sufficient explanation of the creation; that he is at work and hence revealed in the whole of it and in every detail of it; and that he is faithful and consistent so that he always acts *like himself* as a " faithful Creator " and not like a fumbling and interfering artificer. Of course the Scriptures do not envisage a series of secondary causes such as we know. On the other hand, however, they are very clear that both in what *we* should call such secondary causes (that is, the run-of-the-mill occurrences in the world) as well as in those events which seem somehow more directly to manifest what he is " up to " in his world (which *we* would be obliged also to describe in terms of some series of causes), God is not only at work but is also revealed — he expresses himself in the world by what he brings to pass, or allows to come to pass, within it.

Doubtless such a world view raises enormous problems, especially in respect to what we call " evil " in all its aspects. But despite these problems the main assertion stands firm: that God is *there* and that even those aspects of the creation which seem to us contrary to the good and the true and the lovely are somehow held within his power and will in the end be " turned to his praise." Religiously, that conviction is stated in a great word from the Authorized Version, in the book of Job, mistranslated as it is, yet true to the Biblical insight, " Though he slay me, yet will I trust in him."

It is in a world like that, then, that the Christian envisages man's existence, sees him as a creature, made for a purpose, made for community, compact of mind and body in one organic unity, seeking the fulfillment of which sexual love is a sign, in defection from his true self but yet restored in Christ to the wholeness that is purposed for him in the divine intention and that is his eternal destiny. It is against the background of such a conception of the world that a consideration of the problem of human freedom must take place. To that consideration we now turn our attention.

A discussion of human freedom ought to include, for the Christian, two factors. The first is the general question of freedom as such, without special regard for the Christian contribution, and the second is the specifically Christian point of view. Some people would say that this is a mistaken procedure; they would insist that it is only from within the Christian community of faith that the matter can be discussed at all. This position, I think, is both unrealistic and absurd; it is unrealistic because it refuses to recognize that the question of freedom is a vital and inescapable one for those who do not share the Christian faith, live the Christian life, or understand the Christian perspective; it is absurd because it seeks to place the specifically Christian point of view out of all relationship to more general considerations, and therefore makes that point of view utterly irrelevant to the situation of the ordinary human being. Hence we shall deal *first* with more general aspects and *then* proceed to the specifically Christian position. For while Christianity does not look at freedom from a standpoint entirely *de novo,* it has its own unique contribution to make both to the problem in itself and also to any solution that may be offered to the problem. Freedom, for the Christian man, begins with a common experience known to all men; it goes on to include data that are available only for those who look at freedom in the light of the particular affirmations of the Christian faith.

The claim to human freedom presents to the philosopher a problem with which he must wrestle manfully, especially if he is in the tradition of those thinkers who have been seriously influenced by the apparent determinism of the natural order. It presents an equally difficult problem to those whose world view implies what we might call a voluntaristic monism, that is, the belief that there is one supreme and determining will, the will of God, which so rules the world that the wills of created beings have little or no potency in the total scheme of things. But on the other hand, the ordinary man or woman, in his ordinary daily affairs, always seems to assume without question that he is free, that his choice in the last resort is not determined by anything or anybody outside himself, and that he is personally responsible for the acts which, he believes, he freely performs day after day. And because the ordinary man has both this sense of freedom and this sense of moral responsibility, he will most often believe that he actually is free — even if he has never even heard the name of the great moral philosopher, Bishop Joseph Butler, who in the eighteenth century insisted that since we all *assume* that we are free and *act* as if we were free, the most likely hypothesis is that in fact we *are* as we assume ourselves to be.

I am not concerned to argue at any length about the question of human freedom, since I am inclined to agree with Dr. Samuel Johnson that while all argument is *against* it, all experience is *for* it. The reason for this is probably that in argument we are looking back at the past, where we can usually see connections which in the immediacy of experience are not known to us. Chains of cause and effect seem very clear in the retrospective glance, while in the present moment we are more likely to think of the possibilities that appear open to our choice. My own philosophy, apart from the religious convictions that I hold, is based on the assumption that experience rather than abstract theory is the best clue to significant truth. However compelling a theory may appear to be, it cannot provide much of a guide to action; and I am inclined to think that argumentation does not get one very far on matters of such " existential " import as freedom.

This is to say that I agree with those who feel that there is something valid in the experienced fact of freedom. But what do those of us who talk in this way really mean when we say this? Perhaps our freedom, however *real* it may be, is not exactly the *sort* of freedom that has often been claimed. For example, is there in fact any such thing as freedom of the *will* — as distinguished from freedom of choice?

I do not believe that there is any such thing as free *will*. The idea that there is rests upon a quite mistaken conception of the workings of human psychology, a conception that is untrue to our own experience. The human will acts in us as the *motor*, as we might put it, which makes any action possible for us; it is the power or the drive to do this or that. But if we engage in a little elementary introspection, looking into our own living experience when we are conscious of acting with what we feel to be freedom, we seem to see that once we have made a *choice,* decided for this or for that, looked at it with desire and come to the point of actually *wanting* it, the will is then set in operation, triggered like a gun, and hence is no longer free at all. Our will is determined by the strength of our desire for an object — of our appetition, as some moral philosophers would put it — rather than free in and of itself. The direction of the will and its potency are dependent on deep emotional factors, the strength of our desires, and general considerations of personal habit which do, or do not, make us able to put all of ourselves into our action in this or that direction.

Thus the place where we human beings really have freedom is in our *choosing,* in our selection of that which we shall desire, rather than in the conative drive of human personality which is what we mean by the will. When Augustine talks of *liberum arbitrium* he is saying just this: it is in our choosing, in our selection of that upon which we shall concentrate our attention and focus our desires, that we possess freedom. Here we have the capacity to turn our attention, to fix our hearty desires, upon this or that possibility; and what we thus choose will sooner or later become that toward which we act. Our volition will express itself in *that* direction.

But how are we thus free in our choosing? Here again there is a problem. For that which we may like *now* is largely bound up with that which we have liked in the past. We are not entirely and utterly free, with no restrictions of any kind or at any point in our lives. We have already created in ourselves, by our previous acts of choice, a certain " set " or " bent " of desire, which goes largely to determine whether this or that particular possibility will seem attractive to us. Nor is it only our conscious acts of choice which help to build up this " set " or "bent." Our general line or style of life or personality is also molded by our leisure thoughts, our accumulated interests and fancies. To take as example the one factor of leisure thoughts: it has often been said that these " dye " our personality in such a way that it cannot help acting in this or that fashion. We all know how true this is. It is one reason for the agelong insistence that men's leisure time must be spent in some constructive rather than in some destructive manner; that, for instance, the man whose leisure is devoted to vulgar or obscene thoughts will sooner or later find himself unable to enjoy and follow what is " pure " and " lovely " and " of good report." We are being " formed," patterned, molded, shaped, by the things to which our attention wanders when we are not otherwise occupied.

It is also true that in many ways our freedom of choice is seriously limited. All our daily living, in all its phases, is nothing but the building up of a pattern of *self*-determination. The limits that are set on our freedom spring largely, although not exclusively, from that pattern; and there is a deep sense in which the truest freedom may be thought of as nothing else than self-determination — it is the result of the past choices which have made us what we are. The saint will always act in *this* way; the vicious man will always act in *that* way — or if this is too strong, there is at least a high degree of predictability about the general direction in which the one and the other will make a choice among various possibilities that are open before him.

The fallacy of much so-called libertarianism was that it forgot these highly important and very obvious facts about man's experience. And that kind of thought was guilty of still another error, equally contrary to experience. It tended to forget that there are social factors and "natural" aspects of our environment that also limit the extent of our freedom of choice. A child who is brought up in a certain kind of environment — say, in the slums of a city — is not free to choose in the same way as a child who is brought up in another kind of environment — say a garden suburb. A person living in the Sahara Desert cannot choose in the same way as someone living in the Rocky Mountains. The whole situation in which as men we inevitably find ourselves limits our freedom to a greater or less degree. Furthermore, the past history of our society and its accumulated traditions play their part also in establishing the limits within which we choose freely.

So we could go on multiplying the number and extent of the limitations to the freedom which we yet know and experience. But these limitations do not deny the *reality* of our freedom, as some people have foolishly thought; what they do, rather, is *define* our freedom and establish the areas in which we are really possessed of it. In addition, they help us to see that the really important question is not the particular degree of freedom we may have nor the extent of the limitations which may be put upon it. The question that matters most to each and all of us is, What use do we make of such freedom as we do in fact possess?

We can, if we wish, let our fancy play upon that which is not *natural* to us as human beings. When I say "natural" I do not mean here what simply happens to be done by the majority of our fellows; I mean by "natural" that which is in accordance with our nature as men. We have already remarked, in our chapter on human defection, that while it is *natural* for a cat to behave like a cat, it is not natural for a man to do so. Many of us have so let our

attention focus on " cattiness " that we seem to our neigh-
bors to merit that description: " He's a cat." You can select any animal you wish and say the same: a dog, a snake,
a jackass, an opossum, a tiger. We speak of certain qualities that probably wrongly we attribute to these animals;
in them, this or that quality seems to us perfectly right
and proper. But when a man acts in that way, it is not
right and proper; it is not natural to him.

We are meant to be " authentic " human beings, fulfilling ourselves and realizing ourselves as men. This implies
that there is a norm or standard in terms of which we are
enabled to judge whether or not a particular set of desirings, choices, attentions, is natural to us as men. It is precisely at this point that the Christian will introduce one of
the elements in his understanding of the significance of
Jesus Christ. Here, the Christian will insist, is the norm or
standard for human life.

Now I do not wish to be misunderstood in this matter.
I am not suggesting that we are intended to mimic exactly
what Jesus said and did in his own time and place. To
demand this would be a denial of whatever freedom we
possess. What I am saying is that the *essential spirit* of
Jesus Christ, the true center of his human desiring and
attention, can be taken as norm or standard. Christian
experience for nearly two thousand years has insisted on
this as the meaning of " the imitation of Christ," and that
same experience tells us that such " imitation " is a genuine possibility for men and women today. If we learn to
know him through meditation, through prayer, through
communion, through letting our attention focus on him
as he is portrayed for us in the Gospels, this essential spirit
of his humanity can become our freely chosen norm of human life and authentic manhood, and hence the clue to

what *we* shall seek to be and to what *we* shall seek to do. And with that selection, on our part, of the norm which we would make our own, there can come a quickening of our own powers as we set our hearts and direct our thoughts on him and his center of choice. All this explains why it is an agelong and demonstrated part of Christian devotion to turn one's thoughts to him — to read about, to think deeply upon, to direct the affections toward, his life as it is portrayed for us in the Gospels, until his Spirit comes alive in our spirits and we begin to reflect, in however slight measure, his kind of choosing, his way of attending, his sort of selectivity. In the New Testament phrase, we become men " in Christ." Then it is that the great words of the Prayer Book collect have their meaning: we find that his " service is perfect freedom."

But we are not to think that this is done quickly, without thought or effort. It takes time, as we have seen; like everything worthwhile, it requires effort. It is the work of a lifetime to conform our desiring to the desiring which is " the mind that was in Christ Jesus." Furthermore, because this " mind " is personal — that is, embodied in a human life and not some abstract idea of what is good for man to choose — it demands personal surrender or commitment. Abstract moral ideas are all very well, but experience seems to show that they are not likely to " deliver the goods." But the incarnation of moral goodness in a personal life, to which we can make a continuing and ever-renewed response and dedication, gives us concreteness, vividness, and focus. On the other hand, it demands from us a real effort of response, a real concentration of attention, and a real and intentional centering of desire.

Yet the perhaps surprising thing is that the genuine Christian cannot think of this as *nothing but* his own effort. He must indeed work out his "salvation with fear and trembling"; still he knows that all the while "it is God which worketh in . . . [him] both to will and to do of his good pleasure." In this paradox of divine grace and free human response is the whole mystery of the Christian life. It is not sheer mystery, however, for in his own fashion and degree the paradox is known to anyone who has been deeply in love and found himself both empowered and liberated by his responsive commitment to the loved person. As Augustine once said, in speaking of grace, " He who has loved will understand."

All this is included when that same Augustine spoke of the way in which our *liberum arbitrium* (our free choice, with whatever limitations may be set upon it) can become *liberatum arbitrium* (a freed choice). What is that " freed choice "? It is real fulfillment, perfect freedom — the freedom that is given when one is utterly and entirely desirous of the supreme and all-inclusive good, the *summum bonum,* the good which is *the* Good, God as he makes himself known to us in his purpose for the world and for his human children. I should not wish to defend all, or even the major portion, of Augustine's development of this theme; certainly, as I have said earlier, I should not wish to defend his conception of man as a " mass of perdition " or his view of " original sin " as totally laming man and making him impotent ever to choose any good that is *really* good. Augustine's ideas on these matters were much more the results of his *own* special personal experience, and so true for *him,* than the results that would follow from a wider analysis of *all* human experience, and so true for *everyone.* But Augustine's statement of the possibility of the transformation of simple freedom of choice into the kind of choosing which is freed from narrow and distorted

self-determination is correct and true. It is confirmed in
the experience of countless men and women who have
" grown in grace " as they have grown in age and thus have
approached the goal of true fulfillment as men.

But are we ever thus fulfilled while we are *peregrini et
viatores* (pilgrims and wayfarers) here in this world of
time and space? Augustine himself considered this question and answered it by saying that such fulfillment was
possible but unlikely. There is in us so much of *wrong* self-
determination, not to speak of the limiting factors to
which we have referred, that it appears extremely unlikely
that most, if any, of us can attain such fulfillment in this
present stage of our existence. One of the reasons we may
give for our belief in the eternal Kingdom of God — the
heavenly society of charity in self-surrender to the good
which is God — is exactly this lack of fulfillment in the
complete sense here and now. The God who has made us
for such greater freedom and for fulfillment in that freedom is not unreasonably believed to be the God who will
guarantee the realization of the purpose for which he has
made us. Man needs eternity for his truest fulfillment,
known in the freedom that comes when he is liberated
from lower choices and bound to the good that is supreme
and utterly satisfying for him and his fellows.

In the Prayer Book collect for the Fourteenth Sunday
after Trinity, the worshiper asks that he may desire that
which God promises and love that which God commands.
That is what we have been talking about throughout this
chapter. Our true freedom *is* to desire God's promises; it
is to love that which we see his purpose in the world to be,
that which (in the Prayer Book phrase) " he commands."
The result of such desiring and loving, as another collect
phrases it, is that we may have our " hearts set where true

joys are to be found." By the increase in us of faith, hope, and charity, by the growth in us of a deep devotion to the things that truly and rightly make us men, we are put in the way to being fulfilled in freedom and so enabled to live authentically as men; and the end is eternal life.

Beginning from the common experience of freedom of choice, we move toward the kind of freedom that is not found in libertarian license but rather in the supreme act of self-determination in, by, with, under, and through the good which is God himself. To be determined by love for God and his will and ways is to be determined in the highest degree; and thus to be determined is in fact to be truly free. For as Augustine also wrote, in words that we have quoted and discussed many times in these pages, " Thou hast made us to move toward thee, O God, and our hearts " — our desirings, our lovings, our attentions, our concerns — " are unquiet " — disordered, distorted, twisted — " until they rest in or are set upon thee."

The secret of it all is love — not cheap sentimentalism, not vulgar passion, but love — positive, creative, outgoing, sharing goodness. Thornton Wilder, at the end of *The Bridge of San Luis Rey*,[43] spoke of love as " the only survival, the only meaning." To that love we must respond; we must let ourselves be grasped by it, owned of it, used to the limit in its service. So we must take a risk. There is a fine sonnet by S. R. Lysaght, a forgotten poet of the first years of this century, which says all this:

> If Love should count you worthy, and should deign
> One day to seek your door and be your guest,
> Pause! ere you draw the bolt and bid him rest,
> If in your old content you would remain.
> For not alone he enters; in his train
> Are angels of the mists, the lonely quest,

Dreams of the unfulfilled and unpossessed,
And sorrow, and life's immemorial pain.

He wakes desires you never may forget,
He shows you stars you never saw before,
He makes you share with him, forevermore,
The burden of the world's divine regret.
How wise you were to open not! and yet
How poor, if you should turn him from the door.[44]

10

Man the Moral Being

There are three important matters that are left over from our last chapter. They follow immediately upon the recognition that man is a moral being, with responsibility for his choices, when this recognition is linked as closely as we have suggested with the wider considerations of man's religious response to his world. The three matters to which I refer are these: A. What is the relationship of man's moral nature and his moral life to the religious response which is basic to his fulfillment? B. Is there not a danger either of man's religious faith detaching him from his proper concern for his responsibilities in the immediate present *or* of his moral sense seriously diminishing his ultimate concern for final fulfillment in God? C. Is it possible for men really to live as moral beings, obedient to their awareness of the divine purpose for them, in a world in which it seems obvious that accommodation and compromise are required if life is to be lived at all? To these questions we turn in this concluding chapter.

A

A story will be useful as a beginning for discussion of the relation of religion and morality. One day, runs the tale, a Protestant minister and a Roman Catholic priest

met on a village street. In the course of their conversation
it developed that they had different ideas of their ministe-
rial function, ideas that were expressed in the phrases attributed to each of them. " My job," said the Protestant,
" is to try to make good people religious." " Mine," said
the Roman Catholic, " is to try to make religious people
good."

Now, however one may like or dislike the particular
" distribution of terms " in this story, the point that it
makes is a significant one. That point is that there is a
real distinction and yet a close relationship between religion and morality. This point is frequently obscured, especially in a religion like Christianity, in which the moral
consequences of religion are so integral to the whole picture that they are sometimes identified with the thing itself.
But the fact is there, and it needs to be stressed, because we
can never be satisfied with an unethical religion or with
an irreligious morality.

In a day now somewhat long past, there was a movement
for the rewriting of the creeds in what were called " moral
terms." It was felt that the ancient creedal formulas were
unfortunate in that they did not stress sufficiently the
ethical element in religion. But Dr. William Temple, the
late Archbishop of Canterbury, in discussing this idea,
gave the proper answer when he said that a creed that was
solely concerned with ethics would be a creed that developed hypocrites — people who claimed moral goals
which in fact they did not attain. The function of a creed,
he remarked, was to state the revelation of God and our
belief in it; the ethical consequences should follow as a
matter of course, but they were not part of religious belief
as such.

Likewise, long before Temple made these comments,

the Baron von Hügel, in his discussion of the nature of religion, protested that it was concerned with " isness," not with " oughtness," with the reality of God and with the recognition of God by his creatures and not with their moral obligations in the light of that reality and its recognition. Morality, he insisted, is different from religion, although in the highest religions it is closely connected with, and inescapably involved in, the properly religious life. But religion for the Baron was primarily " adoration "; morality was primarily " obligation." Recognition of the validity of this distinction does not in any way militate against the conviction that the divine judgment upon man is finally in terms of total behavior, rather than of specific religious response. Doubtless religion is not important to God in himself; *he* does not have one! His judgment upon men will be concerned with the whole course of their lives, and especially with the integrity, purity, and honesty that does or does not mark them. But for us men, religion is very important; *we* must have one. We must have one because the condition of our right and wholesome living — and hence, ultimately, of our moral behavior — is our attitude toward, and our apprehension of, the total scheme of things such as will give meaning and dignity to human existence. And this, religion, in the long run, is alone able to give.

There is a very immediate and practical reason for this insistence on the distinction between religion and morality — a reason that ought to be obvious in our own day and in our own culture. For a long time, now, the ordinary Anglo-Saxon has tended to identify Christianity with a certain ethical standard. That standard has been understood in one or the other of two ways; one is the rather negative ethic of an older generation that still exerts a powerful influence. Someone has characterized it as the "Don't drink — don't smoke — don't dance morality." The other is the positive but more general ethic of a younger generation, a morality that might be characterized as the "Do good and serve others morality."

But vast numbers of people are unable any longer to accept the first ethic; and we cannot blame them for rejecting such a negative position. Toward the second they often take the attitude of admiration for its intention but wonder about its actual helpfulness in concrete situations. In either case, they have so identified this morality with Christianity that they feel that if they cannot actually attain to such an ethical standard, negative or positive, they have no right to a religion at all, or at least to the Christian religion. Furthermore, they tend to criticize those who are members of the various religious communions on the sole ground that these professing Christians do not fully follow the ethic which is supposedly *identical* with Christianity itself. Professing Christians also are sometimes doubtful as to their right to continue to call themselves Christians, when they must honestly acknowledge that their behavior is all too often below that which ideally is required of them.

It is plain to any historian of religion that in North America the general view of religion follows the "sect" rather than the "church" type, to use Troeltsch's convenient distinction. The sect type regards religion as something for the special and holy *few,* who can claim to be perfect followers of their chosen way, rather than for the sinful *many,* who find help toward goodness and incentive toward moral effort within a fellowship that as a matter of fact has come into existence on quite other grounds. The latter, or church view of religion, regards the fellowship not as " a museum for saints," but as " a hospital for sinners," as the old slogan put it, and rejects the notion that moral uprightness is the implied " condition " of membership. But it is still popular in North America to take the sect view, even if in recent times the ideal has broken down and " the saints " seem fewer in number!

Historically, however, it seems there can be no question that Christianity throughout its long development has not been in the first instance a moral system. Morality has been extremely important, but the *first* emphasis has been put elsewhere. Christianity has been a " religion," centered in the action of God in Jesus Christ. It has been understood as the response in faith and worship to that figure; the dedication of life to him and the empowering of life by him; the transfiguration of personality by his active love and the establishment of a hope for eternal life with God because of Christ's victory over death and sin. It has been a religion embodied in a community, in which the action of God in Christ has been proclaimed down the centuries and made a vitalizing reality for succeeding generations. It has been a religion therefore in which community replaces individualism — of which the Bible itself has been a parable, for it begins with man alone in a garden and ends with man in a city, as one of a company of redeemed brethren.

The result of this religion, in its communal expression, has been a morality that is both humanist and rigorist, both generous and exacting. But the general trend of the Christian movement has been to find the Christian ethic a real and practicable one for men in the degree to which they have truly and wholeheartedly belonged to the fellowship, and not vice versa. As Dr. Harry Emerson Fosdick once expressed it, Christianity has said that " we *ought,* because we *are*." We ought to act like Christians, because by the divine action we have become and now are Christians, that is, we are of the company of disciples and servants of the Lord Jesus Christ.

It is my own conviction that the questing, ill-adjusted, unsatisfied people of our day will be won to Christianity by this kind of approach rather than by the strictly ethical one. But for those within the Christian fellowship, on the other hand, a stirring to action of a moral sort is essential. They need to be roused to a realization of the ethical demands of the faith they profess and the worship they offer. For the others, who have yet to be brought to Christianity, the primary task is to present it as a faith, which makes sense of life, gives dignity to life, and provides power for life. We should welcome them into the fellowship, not because they are morally good but because they are religiously lost. We should preach our faith as God's gospel of deliverance from alienation and lostness and as the assurance that " underneath are the everlasting arms " and the promise that " all shall be well," as Mother Julian of Norwich said, because " God made, God loves, and God keeps " his world. Then, when they have been won to the faith in Christ, we can be both rigorous in the moral demands which that faith makes, and also humanist in recognizing that men are weak and not only may but will sin; in other words, that they will often fail to achieve the kind of living which is natural to " the man in Christ."

We have long been delivered from the idea that ecclesiasticism is the Christian religion, although we now know that the *ekklēsia,* the church, is fundamental to it. We have lately been delivered from the idea that Biblicism is the Christian religion, although we all know that the Bible is the central, classical, and normative expression of our faith, given in terms of its origin and its formative period. We ought also to be delivered from the idea that ethicism is the Christian religion, even while we insist that a wide and high and deep morality is implicit in the faith in Christ.

All men are implicitly religious, even if they do not possess in a marked degree the so-called religious instinct. By this I mean that all men have a desire to make sense of their lives, to ground their being upon the " unconditioned," to be related to the fundamental " drive " in the universe. They may not express this in narrowly religious ways; it is, nonetheless, the only adequate explanation of their existence and their behavior, as Dr. Tillich has so admirably shown in *The Religious Situation*.[45] On the other hand, men do not naturally and immediately apart from participation in the religious community achieve a morality that is consonant with high religion. That is why the Roman priest's remark quoted at the beginning of this chapter is more accurate than the comment of the Protestant minister: " My job," said the priest, " is to try to make religious people good." But there is no reason whatever that the Roman Catholic Church should be allowed to make this claim exclusively. *All* high religion, Catholic and Protestant, is or should be in a like case. The job of the minister is *first* of all to introduce men to God in his holiness, his love, and his forgiveness. *Then,* and only then, can he rightly and intelligibly talk about moral requirements made by that God. For then, and only then, is the context right for such requirements. It is to those who are within the community of faith that the moral imperative needs to be preached; but it will not have much effect upon us if we are without some real and basic religious adjustment.

It is of the essence of the life of a religious tradition that it be life " in a discipline." That is, ascetic and moral theology and their practical implications are an integral part of the whole Christian as indeed of every other religious complex. This is why in the Catholic communions the sacramental rite of confession and absolution has been important; it is why the Methodists were strongest when they had the old " class meetings "; why the Oxford Groups rediscovered the practice of public confession; and why all vital religion has been concerned to recognize men as sinners, to encourage them to confess that fact, and to give them strength to begin again and again the moral life which their faith demands but their practice so sadly fails to achieve. A distinguished Protestant minister in New York has said frankly that, for want of some such contemporary discipline, vast numbers of religious people are frustrated and " beaten " in their lives. On the other hand, for want of a religious orientation, the moral struggle of the professed " humanist " becomes in its own way a tragic frustration.

No matter how carefully one guards oneself, misunderstanding is aways possible in a discussion of this sort. Therefore let me conclude this section by saying that I am not for a moment denying the moral demands of Christianity, nor suggesting that they are unimportant or negligible. I am insisting on something quite different, something about which Kierkegaard had much to say that is invaluable for us. The Christian faith comes *first;* the morality of the Christian tradition comes *second.* But the second is a *real* second; it comes *directly* after the first. When Kierkegaard remarked that the religious category " dethrones " the ethical as well as the aesthetic categories he did not mean that it annihilated them. Evidently some readers of Kierkegaard cannot understand the difference between the two ideas! He meant precisely what he said: that religion is primary, with morality as an inevitable and necessary corollary. For a Christian, as we said at the beginning, there can be no unethical religion nor irreligious morality. The writer of Hebrews put this, with the proper order of things: "The God of peace, that brought again from the dead our Lord Jesus, that great shepherd of the sheep, through the blood of the everlasting covenant, make you perfect in every good work to do his will, working in you that which is well-pleasing in his sight, through Jesus Christ; to whom be glory for ever and ever. Amen."

B

In much of our current literature there is an increasing emphasis upon what might be called "detachment," as the essential attitude of mind for those who wish to preserve equanimity of spirit in the midst of violent change. And even among some Christians there has been a tendency to advocate flight to the mountains or refuge in the catacombs as the strategy indicated by our present situation. It will be worth our while to examine this point of view, in the light of traditional Christian faith, and in the context of the view of human nature taken in this book.

A profitable approach to this problem will be to take some recent popular writers on this subject and examine their positions.

Aldous Huxley [46] in *Ends and Means* wrote at great length on the need for detachment, and in his novel *Time Must Have a Stop* he developed the same theme in fictional manner. Huxley is always interesting, even when his novels creak with an overwhelming load of ideas; but one may wonder how far his view of human nature really makes sense and, above all, how far his notions of religion are congruous with the Christian position. When he writes in *Grey Eminence* that it was devotion to the historic and crucified Jesus which ruined the politics of his chief character, one may surely comment that he has misinterpreted his evidence. It was not devotion to Jesus that was the difficulty but rather a failure to understand the right relationship between temporal possibility and eternal actuality. Again, in his collection of writings by the mystics, east and west, published under the somewhat misleading title *The Perennial Philosophy,* Huxley maintains that the attempt to mix " committed action " with contemplation is bound to lead to disastrous results; hence, he commends to his readers a mysticism that abstracts itself from commitments and seeks to relate the initiate to " pure being." This author may be regarded, therefore, as one who stands entirely on the side of detachment.

A few years ago Arthur Koestler, the novelist and war correspondent, gave us a remarkably stimulating volume entitled *The Yogi and the Commissar.*[47] Koestler's thesis was that there are two possible directions for human life: one is that taken by the yogi, who stands for mysticism and hence for detachment; the other is the way of the commissar, who stands for complete dedication to the improvement of this world or for unlimited attachment. The difficulties of each position are admirably noted by our author, but in the title essay he is compelled to say that for himself he is " inclined " (he does not go much farther than that) to believe that the yogi has chosen the better part, although he admits that involvement in " political " reality is inescapable. His final suggestion is that the right-thinking man will seek a balance between the two possibilities, but that because of the inevitable selfishness and even sordidness of the sphere of action, he will have, as it were, a "reserved participation." Koestler's position, as we shall see shortly, is closer to Christian thinking than Huxley's.

The view of Gerald Heard,[48] a friend of Huxley and a writer who is severely criticized by Koestler for obscurity and pretentious mystification, is much more plainly on the side of detachment. In a long list of books, most notably in his study entitled *Is God Evident?* Mr. Heard is insistent on the priority of the mystical element and urges that neglect of this, and of the techniques by which it may be cultivated, is responsible for the decline of man during the past century. In this book, as in his earlier works such as *The Code of Christ,* Gerald Heard criticizes contemporary Christianity because in his judgment it has immersed itself in the affairs of the world; in his *The Eternal Gospel* he explicitly attempts to dissociate the *truth* of Christianity from its historical and temporal elements and criticizes certain modern theologians, especially Barth and Brunner and their followers, for singling out precisely these historical elements as the either-or of Christian faith. With Heard we may associate Christopher Isherwood, John van Druten, and others who have contributed to a symposium called *Vedanta for Modern Man.*[49] The essays in this book are all of a piece in their insistence on mysticism to the point of detachment, while Mr. Isherwood's [50] later novels argue the same conclusion, in fictional form.

In brief, one might remark that a considerable strain in our contemporary popular literary world, reflecting a strong feeling on the part of those who more properly may be called the " intellectuals " and closely followed by many who could hardly be classified in this way, is intent upon urging that the only valid solution to life's problems, with their complexity and confusion, is the attitude of detachment from the world. And one must also observe that these writers tend to feel that a religion which is to be possible for modern man must be of this same pattern; hence they criticize historical Christianity, or seek to reinterpret it very radically in this respect, because in their judgment it has been willing to accept attachment as a possible religious attitude.

Now it is fairly plain that the movement toward detachment is the result of disappointment and even despair over the collapse of the hopes and ideals to which the last generation was so profoundly attached. Attachment quite obviously had failed. This failure has always been true in personal experience when men have set their hearts upon complete fulfillment in the here and now. It has become more disturbing for many of our age, as their total commitment to secular interests and concerns has led to dreadful disillusionment. The search for utopia has ended in frustration; utopia is as far away as ever it was and the world seems to move toward destruction and ruin, unless some unexpected event occurs to change its direction. And for every man and woman, there is the inescapable fact of apparent total loss in death, since each of us knows that he must die and leave behind him whatever it has been upon which he has set his heart and to which he has given himself in passionate attachment.

When one is disappointed, and, above all, when a whole generation of men and women meets what looks like total frustration, a violent swing is likely. *From* complete commitment to this world and its ways, *to* complete detachment: it is easy enough to see the mechanism for such a change of attitude. The only safeguard against violent swings of this kind is a steadying reliance upon some wise and settled tradition. Indeed one of the valuable functions of tradition, in every area of human experience, is to check this pendulum tendency in man; absence of a deeply felt and known tradition is largely responsible for the chaotic shift of our own age and generation. So it is that many of our best and most thoughtful minds have swung over to the extreme position of saying that *if* we are disappointed in friends and lovers, in social interests and concerns, in our efforts toward the new and brave world of tomorrow, *if* we do in fact die and lose what this world has given us, then the only possible way of life is a total negation of the world and the adoption of a detached attitude toward all worldly interests and worldly loves — a mysticism that extricates us from *this* world and puts us into some other world where permanence is to be found.

There is nothing wrong with mysticism, if it is properly controlled and checked. And there is a great deal wrong with the kind of involvement in the world of our present experience which is carried to the point of losing all proportion and all sense of genuine significance. By involvement of that sort, one loses even what one esteems, for nothing here continues long " in one stay "; we are not safe in our loving or our living or our striving, if these are confined entirely to the world which passes away, with all its desires and all its demands. But the detachment that denies the world can itself lead only to negation and to retreat; and this is not only cowardly in the face of real and actual dangers and genuine and inescapable problems, but it leaves the situation worse for ourselves and our contemporaries and for our children. Above all, from the Christian perspective, it is a denial of the creation in which, despite all the imperfection and inadequacy of the material, God is working out a purpose of good. It tends to suggest that history is unreal or, if not unreal, then thoroughly unimportant. As Huxley and Heard themselves have recognized, it is an Indian view of life, and it leads — as they do not see — to amoralism, defeatism, even nihilism, qualities that have not produced the best and loveliest things in our human experience.

When the Johannine writer tells us that we are to " love not the world, neither the things that are in the world," we should do well to inquire what he means by " world." He does *not* mean the created order, simply as created order. He *does* mean human society, human affairs, the present order of things, as these are conceived, thought of, and oriented apart from God and his presence, power, and purpose. That is a very different matter. In that sense it is perfectly true that we must not love the world or the things that are in it. On the other hand, there is nothing in Christianity that teaches us that we are not to love the things of the created order when we see them as creatures of God and love them with the love appropriate for creatures of God. They are not to have that kind or degree of attachment which belongs to God alone; neither are they to be hated, denied, or disregarded. They are to be reverenced, loved, used, enjoyed, and sought for, in their proper or " ordinate " fashion. Hence there is a detachment about our attachment to them — as an old Negro woman is said to have remarked, " I wear this world like a loose garment." That is profoundly Christian, while Emerson's remark that he could " get along " without the world is not Christian but supercilious and untrue.

There is something about the new school of detachment that reminds one of the Cloud-Cuckoo-Land in Aristophanes' *The Birds*. Situated between heaven and earth, it was not real at all, but represented an imagined place of retreat for those disappointed about life and not very certain of anything else. One suspects that the kind of religion to which our detachment school calls us does not have faith in God so much as it has a *lack of faith* in anything else, a lack that masquerades as faith in God. For if one has genuine faith in God, it is likely that one will have enough confidence in God's creation to be willing to get considerably mixed up in it. And if one is a believer not simply in an abstract God, but in the God and Father of our Lord Jesus Christ, one will know that God himself got mixed up in his creation, in the human life of Jesus and in all that prepared for and followed that incarnate action. If this is accepted as true, it is impossible for the Christian to run away from the rough, tough, harsh facts — to fly from the world. Rather, he must be like Mother Julian of Norwich, who in her *Shewings of Divine Love* tells us, as we have seen, that she learned from God that she was to love the world because *God* loved it. To love the world in God's love and with God's love is to love it safely. As Augustine long ago said in his *Confessions,* "We only safely love those whom we love in thee; for we can never lose those whom we love in him whom we cannot lose."

In his *Journals,*[51] Kierkegaard writes that the difficulty in "Protestantism, in Lutheranism, and in Denmark" as he knew it was that in giving up the idea of the strictly "religious life," with its monasteries and convents, its monks and nuns, it tended to make the "good" secular life — that is, the honest, upright businessman, the astute administrator, the clever theologian, etc. — the "type" for Christianity. It lost, thereby, what he called "the pinch of salt"[52] which gives its unique tang to Christian living, the sense of the eternal which redeems our relativities from sheer immediacy into some genuine participa-

tion in ultimacy. Kierkegaard's remarks are in point here.
For it is unquestionably true that many of us have tended,
in our own time, to assimilate Christianity entirely to attachment and to lose sight altogether of detachment. This
is as true, incidentally, of much contemporary Roman
Catholicism as it is of non-Roman communions; we are
reliably informed that *most* Roman Catholic lay people
have no interest in the " spiritual life," strictly speaking,
while concern for mysticism, contemplation, and the like,
is confined largely to the monastic and conventual houses.

Now there can be no doubt that we owe much to Huxley, Heard, and others who are recalling us to the importance of techniques that will deepen our spiritual and
hence our moral life. We need today, more perhaps than
anything else — and certainly much more than renewed
appeals for Christian " action " — a careful working out
of a theology of, and a practical guide to, the spiritual and
moral life. But this must be based upon authentic Christian faith, with its involvement in the world and in history; it must be grounded in the incarnation and the atonement, moving *ad divinitatem per humanitatem,* as the
old writers used to say — through the humanity which
God made his own in Christ to the Deity who sustains the
creation. And it must take account of modern man, in his
modern situation, with his modern problems, and seek to
help him, in that given place, to know and love and serve
God. In this fashion, that degree of detachment may be
secured which will make our necessary human and loyal
Christian attachment a safe and right one.

Toward this end, we must welcome the publication in
recent years of new editions of works by the old spiritual
masters. *The Cloud of Unknowing,* William Law's *A
Serious Call to a Devout and Holy Life, Theologia Ger-*

manica, Ramón Lull's *The Lover and His Beloved,* not to speak of the great works like *The Ascent of Mount Carmel* and many others, have lately appeared in attractive new format. This is all to the good. Yet it must be regretted that not so much has been done to provide popular, readable, and workable manuals of prayer, especially those which take people *where they are* and seek to show them the way to fulfillment in God. Perhaps Olive Wyon's *The School of Prayer* and Evelyn Underhill's many little books, such as *The Light of Christ* and *The School of Charity,* are the best that we have, although even in America a few have tried their hand at the task, including quite recently John Casteel and John Coburn.[53]

In any event, the Christian cannot be content to "let the world go by"; nor should he be willing to lose himself so completely in this world and its affairs that he forgets what he is here for, where he is going, and who he is. Perhaps one might say, indeed, that the true Christian disciple is he whose heart is set on God, even while he has learned that the world is here to be worked in and served, precisely because God made it, loves it, and keeps it.

The practical conclusion is that the Christian must love the created order, but only in and under God. He must go all out toward it in his concern and in his caring. He must have a relative attachment to it, work hopefully in it, and give his best efforts to making it more like the city of God, to which — and to which alone — his ultimate attachment is due.

C

In a celebrated passage, Søren Kierkegaard writes that the life of a Christian should be marked by an absolute relation to the Absolute and a relative relation to the rela-

tive.[54] This saying is of a piece with his insistence that the
religious category is primary, while the ethical must take
a second place — a view, as we have noted, that is not
equivalent to holding that the ethical has no place at all.
Kierkegaard's remark seems to many very difficult, at
least in the precise form in which he put it; yet the great
Danish writer has stated a fundamental truth about Christian life that we forget at our peril.

For what it comes to, when we try to put it in simpler
language, is that a Christian is one who has a total and
complete commitment to God, with an absolute obligation to perform the will of God according to the divine
norm for humanity. At the same time, in his attempt to
implement that commitment, he must inevitably make
relative decisions in the light of partial knowledge and
must act in a fashion that can only be described as itself
" relative."

To act relatively, in the light of relative decisions but
against the background of an absolute commitment to a
divine norm, means to recognize, take account of, and live
in accordance with, the limitations, approximations, and
restricted possibilities open to man in the world of space
and time. And this must be done whatever we happen to
think about the other major limiting factor, which is
man's " inherited sinfulness," as Kierkegaard called it,
or " original sin," in the more traditional even if unsatis-
factory phrase. Only in this relative manner can we live
in this world at all.

For several generations, however, the accepted attitude
among many Christians has been rather different. Their
position has been to take one or the other of two possible
views, and the choice between these has been determined
by many extraneous considerations — attitude to Scrip-

ture, acceptance of social pressures, and the like. Some take what might be called the *literalist* view and believe that it is imperative for the Christian to follow without accommodation the exact teaching of Jesus, so far as this is at all possible. Of course this necessarily leads to a certain choosiness in conduct, since some interpret that teaching in one way and some in another. In reaction to this kind of literalism, others take the view that perhaps should be called *idealistic*. This view holds that Jesus enunciated certain great ideals to which we must be dedicated, but that there can be no precise imitation of Jesus in an age that is so different from his.

Now the trouble with both these positions is that they restrict all Christian morality to the teaching of Jesus, no matter how that may be interpreted. Hence they miss the wealth of insight and the accumulated wisdom of the moral tradition of the race, contributing to and corrected by the central figure of Christ himself in the totality of his impact upon the moral consciousness of man but derived fundamentally from his religious significance. This latter conception of Christian morality is in essence the traditional or what we may call the *catholic* view, to which we notice an increasing return, though in their own idiom, by theologians and moralists of all Christian denominations.

What Kierkegaard was trying to do, in this as in nearly every range of his thinking (his thinking about the church is an exception), was to get back to something like this more traditional conception of Christianity. Of course, many will disagree with such an interpretation of Kierkegaard. But it is at least arguable that in innumerable places — and signally in his insistence on the absolute demands of Christianity, yet with his discrimination between absolute and relative — he is seeking in new terms and by

devious ways (as in his castigation of " worldly Lutheranism in Denmark ") to work his way back to a conception
of Christian morality in its relation to Christian faith,
which sounds more like Augustine than like either our
contemporary literalists or our idealists. To be sure,
Kierkegaard is not alone in this. Protestant writers such
as Brunner and Niebuhr and Catholic writers such as
Maritain and Gerald Vann are also seeking a conception of
Christian morality which, while it takes account of the
divine and therefore the absolute norm in Jesus, yet sees
this more particularly manifested in his total religious significance as the divine action for men. Further they have
a deep respect for the moral tradition of the historical
Christian community which allowed for the relativities of
human existence and the inevitable limitations both of
our decisions and of our deeds.

We must find a way in which we can combine a firm
insistence on Christianity's demand, for us today as for
Christians in every age, for a total commitment to God and
an honest recognition, in thought and act, of the necessity
for accommodation, even for compromise. To be a Christian means that one is unreservedly given to God as the
ultimate dependability, the final norm for human action,
in the conviction that God as he is made known to us in
Christ is both our infinite succor and our absolute Lord.
But to live in the world at all means that one must understand that the perfection of things and of deeds is not
immediately realizable here and now, since we live in an
obviously limited sphere of human relationship and in an
obviously finite world.

One of the reasons for the " hope of heaven," in the
Christian scheme, is precisely that, as Robert Browning
put it, " A man's reach should exceed his grasp, Or what's

a heaven for? " There is more in man than this world can either contain or express. We need a " more " in which we can come to be ourselves, and in which our human relationships can reach their fullest and most uninhibited expression, finitude and sin being done away. Here in this world, as Augustine saw, we are but pilgrims; we are *viatores et peregrini* (wayfarers and wanderers), as Aquinas said.

Professor Whitehead, commenting in his *Adventures of Ideas* on the teaching of Jesus, remarked that it is precisely because of his eschatology that Jesus' teaching remains enduringly significant.[55] It is not " conditioned," as the psychologists would put it, by particular circumstances or particular times because it has to do with " the last things " and the way to them. Hence it can be both a goal and a goad for all times and all circumstances. It has about it an absolute quality. This is not only the way in which human life ought to be lived; it is the way human life is lived when it is lived in God's intention. Only in and with God (that is, " in heaven ") can we be ourselves in the fullest sense. Nonetheless, we must live in the here and now, for it is in the here and now that we have been placed by God to fulfill his will. So there must be particular and limited, relative and accommodated, ways in which we can express our absolute and unlimited commitment to him who is our Lord and our salvation.

This is in the realm of theory. But it seems essential to get the theory clear before we begin to talk about practical instances. Otherwise we shall get so bogged down in the minutiae of given problems that we lose sight of ultimate significances — a typical Anglo-Saxon failing. This has been one of the most serious difficulties with much of our talking about Christian morality. Either we dwell so com-

pletely in the realm of the ideal that we forget that there
are real situations, or contrariwise we concern ourselves so
much with particularities that we forget the fundamental
principles that run through them all.

Historic Christianity, intent on exactly this problem of
the absolute and the relative in Christian living, has
worked out a moral theology that is as thoroughgoing, and
in its own way as scientific, as any other study in which the
human mind has engaged. Especially in the Roman Catholic Church there has been a vast accumulation of basic
material; and it is to some of us puzzling that non-Romans
do not utilize these important data. But we must recognize that there are genuine difficulties in doing so. For the
moral theology of the Roman Catholic Church has sometimes taken an inelastic form so that it appears, and is, stiff
and unyielding. In such theology the vitalities of experience are often forced into a kind of Procrustean bed, and
if they cannot somehow be made to fit, so much the worse
for life.

Further, much traditional moral theology has failed to
take account of the findings of psychology and other sciences concerning man's " dynamics." It has neglected the
underlying psychological and physiological mechanisms,
not to speak of the sociological and economic factors that
have so much to do with human functioning. Still another
trouble is in the way in which moral theology has often
been administered and applied, in a fashion so lacking in
charity and so " objective " and " detached " that the victim of it feels that he is a specimen in a laboratory rather
than a living and loving, though sinning, human being.

These are real difficulties. But in the light of our new
insight into the nature of man's moral situation and with
due recognition of the new and immense developments in

our knowledge, there is no reason why the best minds of the Christian church should not get to work. The wisdom of the Christian centuries is at our disposal. It is possible to rethink the moral theology of the Christian tradition in terms of what we know of man, sociologically, physiologically, and psychologically. It is not beyond our power to restate that theology in ways which are alive and not merely formal, to apply its great truths with understanding and sympathy to new conditions. Many years ago Leonard Hodgson, in his inaugural lecture as Regius Professor of Moral Theology at Oxford University, discussed this matter vigorously and suggestively. To the best of this writer's knowledge, his address is the only brief sketch so far available that unites both the theoretical and practical sides of our problem and points the way to a solution.

To give one illustration, let us consider the matter of marriage and divorce. Recent controversies have illustrated all the possible errors about Christian morality. We have had the *literalists* who take what they conceive to be the New Testament position *au pied de la lettre*. We have had the *idealists* who talk about the " ideal of Christian marriage " toward which a married couple is supposed to struggle. We have had the *rigorists,* who apply a traditional conception with no regard for new circumstances. We have had the *libertarians,* who appear simply to accept the fashions of the day without regard for the Christian norm. What we have not had, or have had in far too few instances, is recognition of the absolute nature of God's will for man — that he shall live humanly, in commitment to God and in dependence on his saving power, in the community of his brethren, in the fellowship of the church, with equally serious recognition of the fact that in this world there will inevitably be limited realization of the norm, inevitable failures to see or to carry out the absolute. And along with this failure we have lacked the further understanding that the church must deal sympathetically, comprehendingly, helpfully, with men and women in all the complexity of their human situation.

Our consideration of Christian morality cannot be concluded without a reference, however brief, to what is called strictly "the religious life." Whatever may be thought of monks and nuns, by those to whom this vocation is not familiar, we do have here men and women who, so far as is at all possible in this world, have committed themselves without reserve to God and his will. As Kierkegaard saw, and said so well in his *Journals,* they placard absolute Christianity before our eyes. Absolute poverty, absolute chastity, absolute obedience, are not indeed possible for any man, since he will always own at least his thoughts, always be open to evil suggestions, always be tempted to seek his own way. But the monk and the nun, or any others who in their special ways are thus totally committed, stand in this our relative world for that which is the truth about all life; namely, that the genuinely human way of living is in utter dependence upon, and complete obedience to, the absolute will of God. *That* is ultimate in human fulfillment.

That the monk and nun have chosen this way does not mean that the rest of us are *bad.* The greatest contribution of the "religious" is like the real contribution of the "pacifist by vocation," who, as Reinhold Niebuhr has pointed out, plainly indicates to all men the *inadequacy* of every attempt to live relatively and by compromise. There is a tension here which to some may appear to be a contradiction. But it is in that tension that we find the growing edge of Christian morality.

We may thank God that there is no easy and entirely satisfactory solution of the problems of Christian morality, in theory any more than in practice. Instead there is a chance to think and act, as we live together, growing in understanding because God intends us to use our minds and not to be moral robots. Doubtless we shall often go wrong. Yet our absolute commitment remains; and in and through our sin and our error, we may make our own the words of the Holy Saturday Exultet in the Western liturgy: *O felix culpa, quae talem ac tantum meruit habere Redemptorem!* — " O fortunate fault, which won such and so great a Redeemer! "

Appendix: The Meaning of Words in Worship

We are often told by anthropologists that the distinguishing mark of man, in establishing the *human* as other than the merely *animal*, is his language. Man not only makes sounds; he verbalizes — he orders and arranges sounds as an instrument for conveying significant thought and expressing meaning. In all religions there is such a use of language; and in Christianity, perhaps more than in other religious cultures, language has been a central aspect of the tradition, in proclamation and in adoration. Hence it is appropriate, in a discussion of human nature in the light of Christian faith, to consider the place of words in the peculiarly Christian activity of worship.

Increasingly it is being recognized by Christians of all denominations that the characteristic activity of the whole Christian community, whatever branch of it they may prefer, *is* the action of worship. The revival of interest in, and concern for, the liturgical life of the church is one of the striking facts of our time; and in denominations that for long have tended to relegate the ordering of the worship of the church to a relatively unimportant place on their agenda, there is a new awareness of the distinctive quality and the high significance of the occasion when the community gathers together in prayer and praise.

I have said " the liturgical life of the church "; and this at once raises a question, for many Christian denominations have been unconcerned for, sometimes positively averse to, the idea of liturgical worship. By " liturgy " one means the public action of worship by a community, with the use of prescribed and established forms, thus guaranteeing the possibility of common participation — liturgy is " common prayer," and that requires agreed words and agreed actions, so that the fullest sharing may be possible for those who take part. And in historical Christianity, there can be no doubt, the liturgical action par excellence has always been the Eucharist, the Lord's Supper, the Holy Communion — call it what you will.

During the hundreds of years since the " night in which he was betrayed," the words and actions of Jesus in that upper room, as remembered in the Christian tradition, have come to be put in a setting that has acquired a certain form of structure — what Dom Gregory Dix appropriately called " the shape of the liturgy." [56] The taking of bread and wine, the blessing of them, with the breaking of the bread, and then their distribution to the faithful: here is the " shape "; and with this, there have been associated certain appropriate actions and certain appropriate words. So the Eucharistic action has developed into several groups of fairly established liturgical services.

But it is not only in the Eucharist that such formalization has been found. The same development has taken place in the other rites of the Christian church — in the " choir offices " of daily morning and evening prayer, in litanies, and in other such services. Whether a given denomination centers its worship in the regular Sunday-by-Sunday celebration of the Holy Communion, or for its normal Sunday worship engages in some other form with less-frequent celebrations of the Eucharist, the fact still remains that a certain stylizing is bound to take place and always does take place.

Our concern in this appendix is not with the structure of the services of the church, nor with the actions that are found in connection with those services; it is rather with the language, equally stylized, or with words that are used in the worship of Christian people as that worship expresses itself in the great social rites of the community. For the words that are used in all the liturgies, whether they be the Eucharistic liturgies that have come to us (with modifications from time to time and from denomination to denomination) from the early days of the Christian church, or the forms of service that have their origin in the sixteenth century when the Reformers adopted (and their successors did the same) some other type of traditional worship, have a certain significant and distinctive quality.

In the first place, the words used in our traditions of worship are either Scriptural or are molded by Scriptural language. That fact immediately leads to the observation that they are metaphorical or poetic. The Bible, someone has said, is a great poem about God and man in their relationship one to another. It does not discuss these matters in the conceptual terminology that one might find in philosophical writing; even more obviously, it does not speak in the jargon of the sciences. Biblical language is highly poetical; it is concerned to speak of God and man and of their relationship in images that are drawn from the vitalities of personal and social experience and from the realm of history. Every man naturally speaks as a poet; as we remarked in the main text of this book, despite M. Jourdain in Molière's play who discovered that he had always been talking prose, the fact is that man is always talking poetry. And the more intimate and immediate the experience which is being spoken, the more highly poetical the language used. The lover speaks of "loving with all his heart"; this does not mean something observable and reportable on a cardiograph, but is rather a highly symbolic way of describing a response that neither science nor philosophy as such can express or contain; it is poetry.

Above all is this true of the God-man relationship, for it is necessarily the case that every sentence in which God is the subject of a verb is a metaphorical sentence; if you will, it is "mythological." By this I do not mean that is it a "fairy tale" and has no truth value. I mean that man cannot find words that will describe with scientific precision or philosophical univocity, having exactly the same meaning, vis-à-vis God, as we would expect in discussing matters of common human knowledge, his sense of the presence, the power, and the activity of the divine Reality. He can speak only allusively, suggestively. Furthermore, as the great theologians have always known, even the highest and best words available to us must, when applied to God, have an "analogical quality" — there is always the *O altitudo* of which Sir Thomas Browne spoke in *Religio Medici;* [57] there is always the "eminent" mode of predication in which language appropriate to one level of experience is used of another, against a background of mystery and wonder. That is to say, there is poetry.

Once again, the words of our worship are words of action. Christianity is not a religion of passive quietistic absorption in Deity; it is a religion that speaks of "the mighty acts of God." It is inevitable that the language that speaks of God, and of man in relation to God, shall be language in which God is said to "do" this or that and in which man is said to respond in love, in worship, in penitence, in obedient surrender. But the fashion in which God acts is very different from that which can be described directly in terms of human action; just as when God

" speaks," he does not have a mouth that forms the words that we are accustomed to employ in our human speech relationships. The only way in which we can state what God " says," or describe the ways in which God " acts," is by taking our human experience of speaking and of doing and directing it Godward. But we must be very careful lest we assume that in doing this we have exhaustively or precisely described what we mean when we say that God is doing or saying. Our language again is to be seen as allusive and suggestive — as poetical.

Theologically speaking, all of God's words and deeds toward man are known to us *ad modum recipientis;* that is, they are accommodated to the understanding of the men and women to whom he speaks and for whom he acts. It is equally true that the only way in which we can talk about these words and deeds is by the use of our own human modes of expression; men have no other method if they hope to convey meaning. Augustine said, for example, that we call God Trinity-in-Unity not so much in order to make absolute statements about him, as in order to avoid being silent before the mystery that has been revealed to us concerning God's " inner life " and his relationships with his world.

Again, the words of our worship, whether they are Biblical words or whether they are the hallowed symbolical words that have come to us from and through the whole tradition of Christian faith, worship, and life — words such as " grace," " pardon," " incarnation," " atonement," " redemption," and the many others with which our worship is filled — these words are for us, in Professor Tillich's phrase, " words with power." This is why it is impossible to devise nice, neat, completely up-to-date expressions that will convey with complete exactness and total adequacy the content of the Christian faith. Within the tradition of Christian life, for those who are "initiates," these words and others like them are words that have an allusive and suggestive quality that modern-invented words would not possess.

Certainly it is true that these words constitute a considerable obstacle for the outsider who has not been admitted to the secret heart of the community's life; and that involves the Christian in a tremendous and difficult apologetical task; the discussion has occupied the time and attention of many great Christian scholars. But the main point remains inescapable. Whatever may be the difficulties, our language in worship is of necessity traditional, as it is of necessity poetical and imaginistic; and we are wishing for the impossible when we wish to avoid or escape this fact.

The result of this situation is that the words of our worship have what we have learned to call a "numinous" character. That means that they have the capacity to convey meaning, subtly, poetically, by allusion and by suggestion, and thus to attract us and move us in the depths of our being; while at the same time they have a mysterious power by which they put us in awe and make us understand that the ways of God and his will for men can only be apprehended "with fear and trembling." Exactly the same character is found in the things "done" in the great liturgical tradition of Christianity; and this explains why the ancient rites and ceremonies of the church have such a wonderfully evocative as well as such a strikingly impressive quality about them.

There are two consequences that are worth noting. The first is that the only really effective way of altering the worship of the Christian church is not by radical surgery nor by complete renovation, but by gradual change and by the slow but sure assimilation of new ideas and new phrasing of ideas which can only come when the faithful worshipers are introduced little by little to new ways of saying the old things. The attempt to create, brand-new, some liturgy or service of worship, in which the contents will be simple and clear, almost inavariably results in an impoverishment of worship and a cheapening of its forms. But yet there can be change as there has been much change indeed, over the centuries. Change is possible, although it must always come in slow, patient, and humble ways.

The second consequence of what we have said is that we need always to distinguish carefully between liturgically apt language and the more precise terms of theological definition. For example, we can speak of God's " pouring his grace into our hearts " (in the words of an ancient collect) , but we are not to think that grace is like a fluid that is " poured " into men by God. Or again, we can speak in our worship of God's " coming down," or of Christ's " ascending far above all heavens," but we must not take these phrases as if they were theologically precise in a spatial kind of sense. One of the unhappy results of the theological revival in our own day, associated with " neo-orthodoxy " in all forms, is that there is tendency in some circle to think that the poetic and metaphorical and symbolical (and I am not here attempting a careful discrimination in the use of these words) idiom of our devotion and worship, like that in which we speak of our psychological experience of the meaning of redemption, shall be taken for an appropriate theological description. When we say, rightly enough, that " the circle of man's self-centeredness," his being *incurvatus in se,* as Luther put it, must be " broken into by the divine action," we ought not think that this is a theologically and ontologically accurate statement of what happens. Neither are we to assume that the liturgical and Biblical language that speaks of God's " coming into the world " is to be taken literally as a description of the incarnation. Theologically, ontologically if you will, " the emergence of the divine Word in the humanity of Jesus Christ " may very well be a much better way of describing what in our worship we describe in the words: " who for us men, and for our salvation, came down from heaven." Admittedly " emergence " is also a metaphorical word — as indeed all words are metaphorical; but for us today it may be theologically appropriate in a higher degree than the more traditional liturgical word.

What is wanted is not so much a *de*-mythologizing of the language of our worship, nor even a *re*-mythologizing of it. The former is impossible since we necessarily think in terms of the metaphorical and the poetical; the latter is undesirable, since the " words with power " have become so much a part of our tradition that we can hardly do without them. What is wanted is an *in*-mythologizing or an entrance into the poetic and mythological spirit which is in this language, a feeling for its depths of meaning and an assimilation of that meaning into our own lives. It is after that entrance, in the dimension of depth, that we shall then be able to go ahead with the task of rethinking and restating, for theological purposes, the truths that are there disclosed. We must make that effort of restatement, in terms of our own patterns of thought, scientific as well as philosophical; but we shall not do ourselves or the Christian church a service if we throw out, in a purely contemporaneous spirit, the language of our worship, in all its poetry, its mystery, its depth, and its power.

Notes

1. Canto lxxxi, p. 99, *The Cantos of Ezra Pound.* Copyright 1934, 1948, by Ezra Pound. Reprinted by permission of New Directions.
2. Alfred North Whitehead, *Adventures of Ideas* (Cambridge University Press, London, 1935), p. 170.
3. Ernest Hemingway, *For Whom the Bell Tolls* (Charles Scribner's Sons, 1940).
4. Friedrich von Hügel, *Essays and Addresses,* Vol. II (J. M. Dent & Sons, Ltd., London, 1926), p. 62.
5. William James, *Psychology — Briefer Course* (Henry Holt & Company, Inc., 1905), p. 6.
6. J. W. Harvey, *Philosophy* (November, 1944), pp. 195–215.
7. Thomas Aquinas, *Summa Theologica* II. lxxxiii. 12; II. lxxxiv. 2; II. lxxxv. 1.
8. I am indebted to my colleague Prof. Sydney Barr for assistance in this " Note," although he is of course not responsible for my use of his material.
9. Hugh of St. Victor, *De Sacramentis* (quoted in M. B. Stewart's *Dogmatic Theology Outline,* printed by The General Seminary Bookstore).
10. Hastings Rashdall, *Christus in Ecclesia* (T. & T. Clark, Edinburgh, 1904), p. 42.
11. Augustine's definitions are cited from M. B. Stewart's *Outline* (see note 9).
12. *Summa Theologica* I. i. 8.
13. *Ibid.,* II. lxxxiv. 2.

14. Walter Lowrie, *The Church and Its Organization* (Macmillan & Co., Ltd., London, 1912), *passim*.

15. Dietrich von Hildebrand, *Liturgy and Personality* (Longmans, Green & Co., Inc., 1943).

16. Evelyn Underhill, *Man and the Supernatural* (E. P. Dutton & Company, Inc., 1928), p. 166.

17. Alfred C. Kinsey, Wardell B. Pomeroy, and Clyde E. Martin, *Sexual Behavior in the Human Male* (W. B. Saunders Company, 1948).

18. François Mauriac, *Woman of the Pharisees*, tr. by Gerard Hopkins (Henry Holt & Company, Inc., 1946).

19. Augustine, *De Civitate Dei* XIV. xxviii.

20. Jean-Paul Sartre, *Being and Nothingness*, tr. by Hazel Barnes (Philosophical Library, Inc., 1956).

21. *Ibid.*, p. 615.

22. D. H. Lawrence, *Lady Chatterley's Lover* (Grove Press, 1959).

23. Martin Jarrett-Kerr, *D. H. Lawrence and Human Existence* (Philosophical Library, Inc., 1951).

24. Albert Camus, *The Plague*, tr. by Stuart Gilbert (Modern Library, Inc., 1948), p. 197.

25. James Barr, *The Semantics of Biblical Language* (Oxford University Press, London, 1961).

26. Launcelot Andrewes, *Preces Privatae* (Methuen & Co., Ltd., London, 1903), p. 169.

27. Roland Mushat Frye, *Perspective on Man* (The Westminster Press, 1961), pp. 122–123.

28. F. R. Tennant, *The Concept of Sin* (Cambridge University Press, London, 1912).

29. Charles Sherrington, *Man on His Nature* (Cambridge University Press, London, 1946).

30. Robert L. Calhoun, *What Is Man?* (Association Press, 1939).

31. James Matthew Thompson, *Through Fact to Faith* (Edward Arnold, Ltd., London, 1912), pp. 112–113.

32. William Scott Palmer, *Diary of a Modernist* (Edward Arnold, Ltd., London, 1910), pp. 174–177.

33. Dorothy M. Emmet, *Function, Purpose, and Power* (Macmillan & Co., Ltd., London, 1957), pp. 221–222.

34. Robert H. Bonthius, *Christian Paths to Self-Acceptance* (King's Crown Press, 1948).

35. From *Collected Poems of Gerard Manley Hopkins,* ed. by W. H. Gardner (Oxford University Press, 1948), p. 111. Used by permission.

36. Alfred Edward Taylor, *The Faith of a Moralist,* Vol. II (Macmillan & Co., Ltd., London, 1930), p. 125.

37. Mother Julian of Norwich, *Revelations of Divine Love* (Methuen & Co., Ltd., London, 1927).

38. J. A. T. Robinson, *In the End, God* (James Clarke & Company, Ltd., London, 1950).

39. Leonard Hodgson, *For Faith and Freedom* (Basil Blackwell & Mott, Ltd., Oxford, 1955–1957).

40. Augustine, *De Civitate Dei* XXII. xxx.

41. *Selected Poems of Robert Browning* (Penguin Books, Ltd., London, 1954), pp. 225–226.

42. Søren Kierkegaard, *The Point of View,* tr. by Walter Lowrie (Oxford University Press, London, 1939), p. 103.

43. Thornton Wilder, *The Bridge of San Luis Rey* (Albert & Charles Boni, Inc., 1927), p. 235.

44. Quoted by B. H. Streeter in *Reality* (The Macmillan Company, 1926), p. 57.

45. Paul Tillich, *The Religious Situation* (Meridian Books, Inc., 1956).

46. The books by Aldous Huxley mentioned in this paragraph are: *Ends and Means* (1937), *Time Must Have a Stop* (1944), *Grey Eminence* (1942), *The Perennial Philosophy* (1945), all published by Harper & Row, Publishers, Inc.

47. Arthur Koestler, *The Yogi and the Commissar* (The Macmillan Company, 1945).

48. The books by Gerald Heard mentioned in this paragraph are: *Is God Evident?* (1948), *The Code of Christ* (1941), *The Eternal Gospel* (1946), all published by Harper & Row, Publishers, Inc.

49. *Vedanta for Modern Man,* ed. by Christopher Isherwood (George Allen & Unwin, Ltd., London, 1952).

50. Christopher Isherwood, *Down There on a Visit* (Simon and Schuster, Inc., 1962).

51. Søren Kierkegaard, *Journals,* ed. by Alexander Dru

(Oxford University Press, 1938) , pp. 711 and 831.

52. *Ibid.,* p. 467.

53. The books referred to are: *The Cloud of Unknowing* (Harper & Row, Publishers, Inc., 1948) ; William Law, *A Serious Call to a Devout and Holy Life,* ed. by John Meister *et al.* (The Westminster Press, 1948) ; *Theologia Germanica,* ed. by Thomas S. Kepler (The World Publishing Company, 1952) ; Ramón Lull, *The Lover and His Beloved* (S.P.C.K., London, 1923) ; St. John of the Cross, *The Ascent of Mount Carmel,* ed. by E. Allison Peers (T. Baker, London, 1922) ; Olive Wyon, *The School of Prayer* (The Westminster Press, 1944) ; Evelyn Underhill, *The Light of Christ* (1945) and *The School of Charity* (1934) , both published by Longmans, Green & Co., Ltd., London; John L. Casteel, *Rediscovering Prayer* (Association Press, 1955) ; John B. Coburn, *Prayer and Personal Religion* (The Westminster Press, 1957) .

54. Kierkegaard, *The Point of View,* p. 164.

55. Whitehead, *Adventures of Ideas,* p. 19.

56. Dom Gregory Dix, *The Shape of the Liturgy* (The Dacre Press, London, 1945) .

57. Thomas Browne, *Religio Medici* (J. M. Dent & Sons, Ltd., London, 1906) .